# Come, Follow Me

# Come, Follow Me

## Becoming Disciples and
## Members of the Body of Christ

### CHRISTOPHER N. WHITE

Thomas E. Lowe, Ltd.
New York
2013

Published in New York, New York, by Thomas E. Lowe, Ltd.

Cover designed by Johnathan Caleb Rivers
Cover photo © 2007 by Daniel H. Voll

**Library of Congress Control Number: 2013931858**
ISBN-13: 978-0-913926-07-9
ISBN-10: 0-913926-07-8

*Printed in the United States of America*

Thomas E. Lowe, Ltd. Web address: *victory4you.net*

*For my Lord and Savior, Jesus Christ,*
*who laid down His life for the sake of His eternal Bride,*
"that He might present her to Himself a glorious church,
not having spot or wrinkle or any such thing, but that she
should be holy and without blemish."
(Ephesians 5:27)

# *Contents*

# *Prologue*

*Picture one.*   Seen through the glass of a giant aquarium, a school of hundreds of fish swirls through the water, a silvery forceful mass of seething vitality. They are many, but move with the decisiveness of one.

*Picture two.*   Seen from the interstate highway on a quiet morning, a large flock of birds moves against the cold blue sky, their motion like the alternating push and glide of an ice skater but in shorter bursts. It is the flock's motion as a whole, not individual birds, that captures the eye. They are many but move as one. Something makes possible a remarkable coordination.

Yet the flock doesn't move like an automaton or a regimented army with strictly linear flight and square turns. It is fluid, alive, with margins constantly in motion. The flock may move in a general direction across the sky, but in getting there, it takes the unpredictable path of a butterfly across a meadow. "The wind blows wherever it pleases. You hear its sound, but you cannot tell where it comes from or where it is going."[1]

*Picture three.*   Seen from the Kebar River in Babylon:

a whirlwind came out of the north, a great
cloud, and a fire infolding itself, and a bright-
ness was about it...

out of the midst thereof came the likeness of
four living creatures.... As I looked at the living creatures, I saw a wheel on the ground beside each creature....

When the living creatures moved, the wheels
beside them moved; and when the living creatures rose from the ground, the wheels also
rose. *Wherever the spirit would go, they would
go,* and the wheels would rise along with
them, because the spirit of the living creatures
was in the wheels.

When the creatures moved, they also moved;
when the creatures stood still, they also stood
still; and when the creatures rose from the
ground, the wheels rose along with them, because the spirit of the living creatures was in
the wheels.[2]

Ezekiel saw a vision of the glory of the Lord, awesome,
wondrous, holy. The expression of that glory in the living
creatures and the wheels beside them speaks to another
mystery.

*Picture four.*

"The body is a unit, though it is made up of
many parts; and though all its parts are many,
they form one body. So it is with Christ....

There are different kinds of gifts, but the same
Spirit. There are different kinds of service, but
the same Lord. There are different kinds of
working, but *the same God works all of them in
all men* ... .

To one there is given through the Spirit the
message of wisdom, to another the message
of knowledge by means of the same Spirit, to
another faith by the same Spirit, to another
gifts of healing by that one Spirit, to another
miraculous powers, to another prophecy, to
another distinguishing between spirits, to another speaking in different kinds of tongues,
and to still another the interpretation of
tongues. All these are the work of one and the
same Spirit, and he gives them to each one,
just as he determines."[3]

How do the individual, separate members of the Church
move as one? In Ezekiel's vision, "When the living creatures moved, the wheels beside them moved...because
the spirit of the living creatures was in the wheels." Paul's
epistle to the Romans draws a similar picture. "You, however, are controlled not by the sinful nature but by the
Spirit, if the Spirit of God lives in you. And if anyone
does not have the Spirit of Christ, he does not belong to
Christ."[4]

Without individual submission to the Lord
and his Spirit, coordination is impossible.

The variety of all creation speaks of the Lord's incred-
ible creativity; it is a mirror of his glory. Did he intend

any less for the Church? No. "His intent was that now, through the church, the manifold wisdom of God should be made known to the rulers and authorities in the heavenly realms."[5] The outline, the shape, the margin of the Flock is constantly in motion, many expressing the One.

If the Lord is not cramped or stereotyped in moving or working, then neither does he intend his Church to be stuck in a rut or constrained by a straitjacket. He made us to be alive, active, moving, and engaged with the world around us. As we walk with him—neither ahead nor behind, but keeping in step through our spirit—he expresses himself through us. As a member of my fellowship once remarked, "Inspiration is *normal.*" Sometimes a banjo's tight drumhead picks up notes from a piano playing nearby and resonates in response, making its strings sing. If we are attuned to the Lord, we can hear what he is saying and express it. "I live in a high and holy place, but also with him who is contrite and lowly in spirit..."[6]

So we are many, yet we are one.

They follow the Lamb wherever he goes.[7]

Prem Thomas
Hamden, CT

# Part I

# Discipleship

# 1   *Believers or Disciples?*

The best description of the Christian life portrayed in the
New Testament is that of discipleship leading to authentic, active membership in the Body of Christ. Therefore,
the first part of this book describes what it means to become a disciple of Jesus. Once we become disciples, however, desiring to do God's will and not our own, then the issue arises of finding our place in the church, Christ's Body.
But what is the church from God's perspective?

In the second part of this book, we will explore the
nature of the New Testament church, as well as what it
means to become a fully functioning member of Christ's
Body—in all the richness of its Biblical dimensions. Paul's
prayer for the saints in Ephesians 3:14-19 was that they
would not be satisfied with only a partial understanding
of their calling in Christ, but that they might enter into the
full dimensions of that calling. We are saved not just so that
we may be freed from the power of sin and escape eternal death in hell, as wonderful as that may be. Rather we
are saved so that we may be transformed into the image of
Jesus, becoming living stones in the Lord's eternal temple
and members of the Bride of Christ:

> For this reason I bow my knees to the Fa-
> ther of our Lord Jesus Christ, from whom the
> whole family in heaven and earth is named,
> that He would grant you, according to the
> riches of His glory, to be strengthened with
> might through His Spirit in the inner man,
> that Christ may dwell in your hearts through
> faith; that you, being rooted and grounded in
> love, may be able to comprehend with all the
> saints what is the width and length and depth
> and height—to know the love of Christ which
> passes knowledge; that you may be filled with
> all the fullness of God.

After the first century AD, much of what Paul describes
here was lost, buried under a sea of false doctrine, tradition, and oppressive hierarchical religion. Believers in Jesus today are beneficiaries of the great Reformation, which
restored much light and truth. Yet in these last days, the
greatest need of all is for *Restoration* of the Scriptural pattern, purity, and power of the church of Jesus Christ.

In our day, the term "believers" is used much more often than "disciples" to describe followers of Jesus Christ.
Yet the word "believers" appears only twice as a noun in
the Greek New Testament, in Acts 5:14 and in 1 Timothy
4:12[1], while the saints are described as "disciple(s)" well
over two hundred times. Are we missing something here?
Have we made an *end* out of what the Bible describes as
only the *beginning* of true spiritual life, coming to believe
in Jesus? Please do note, however, that "believe" as a verb
appears many times in the New Testament, demonstrating
that faith is an action, not just a state of being.

## 1.1 INSTRUCTED IN HIS WAYS

The word *believer* speaks of one who entrusts his or her well-being to Jesus, by faith in Him.[2] A small child can be a believer in Jesus just as fully as an experienced, gray-haired saint. *Disciple*, however, has a deeper meaning. The word first appears in English Scripture as translating the Hebrew word, *limmuday* (plural of למוד, lim-mood), from Isaiah 8:16, "Bind up the testimony, seal the law among my *disciples*." The word refers to one who is instructed, growing accustomed to the ways of his teacher.[3] A disciple is someone who has deliberately set out to know the Lord and His ways, one who walks in the path of God's Word. The author of Psalm 119 is just such a student of the Almighty, as may be seen in verses 10-16,

> With my whole heart I have sought You;
> Oh, let me not wander
>     from Your commandments!
> Your word I have hidden in my heart,
>     that I might not sin against You.
>
> Blessed are You, O LORD!
>
> Teach me Your statutes.
> With my lips I have declared
>     all the judgments of Your mouth.
> I have rejoiced in the way of Your testimonies,
>     as much as in all riches.
> I will meditate on Your precepts,
>     and contemplate Your ways.

> I will delight myself in Your statutes;
> I will not forget Your word....

We tend, even as Christians, to seek worldly riches. But note that the Psalmist rejoices "in the way of Your testimonies as much as in all riches." The Hebrew for "your word" in verse 11, אמרה (im-rawʹ)[4], may be translated as either *word* or *commandment*. There are five other Hebrew words in this passage that also reflect commandment, judgment, or verdict—all describing the authoritative nature of God's word (*mitzváh, chōq, mishpát, piqqúd, dabár*). The teachings of the Lord are eternal and unchanging, and the disciple pays careful attention to them.

The life-long nature of discipleship is clearly shown in verses 111-112. This is no passing fancy or stage of development:

> Your testimonies I have taken
>     as a heritage forever,
> for they are the rejoicing of my heart.
> I have inclined my heart
>     to perform Your statutes
>     forever, to the very end.

One characteristic common to many today is a deep reluctance to commit to *anything*, other than oneself, for more than a short while. Yet here the psalmist speaks of a commitment to God that has no end, no escape clause, no *if*.

In Isaiah 8 the prophet was speaking to an Israelite nation that had so deeply rebelled against the God of Israel that He instructed His prophet to "not walk in the way of this people"—lest he come under the same judgment. Out of all the nations on earth, the Lord had revealed Himself

and His word to Israel. Yet the Jewish people had turned
away from their God. Therefore, the very law that He gave
to Israel for light and life was about to be turned against
them for darkness and judgment:

> But the word of the LORD was to them,
>    "Precept upon precept,
>    precept upon precept,
>    Line upon line, line upon line,
>    Here a little, there a little,"
> That they might go and fall backward,
>    and be broken
> and snared and caught.
> (Isaiah 28:13)

God Himself was about to become,

> "a stone of stumbling and a rock of offense to
> both the houses of Israel, as a trap and a snare
> to the inhabitants of Jerusalem.... Bind up the
> testimony, seal the law among my disciples.
> And I will wait on the Lord, who hides His
> face from the house of Jacob; and I will hope
> in Him."
> (Isaiah 8:14,16–17)

Only true disciples, followers of the Lord, among the Jewish people would continue to understand the testimony or
the law. Why? Because Israel's heart had turned from trust
in the Lord to foreign kings and foreign gods, even to the
point of consulting mediums and spiritists as described in
verse 19. In response, verse 20 declares,

> "To the law and to the testimony:

> if they speak not according to this word,
> it is because there is no light in them." (KJV)

Israel had turned from the light of their God to the darkness of this fallen world, and the Lord hid "His face from
the house of Jacob..." What a fearful precursor of Jesus'
words in Matthew 6:22–23:

> "The lamp of the body is the eye. If therefore
> your eye is good, your whole body will be full
> of light. But if your eye is bad, your whole
> body will be full of darkness. If therefore the
> light that is in you is darkness, how great is that
> darkness!"

In the New Testament, the Greek for disciple, *math-
etes* (μαθητής, mah-thay-tes´)[5], means a learner, a pupil, or
again a disciple. In the early church, becoming a *disciple* of
Jesus was the normal consequence of becoming a believer.
If in our day we often speak of Christians as believers, we
need to remind ourselves that believing and being born
again are only the beginning of the Christian life, not the
end. Becoming a disciple of Jesus is what the Lord intends
for the rest of our lives. The Heavenly Father wants us to
become *life-long learners* from and *followers* of His Son.


1.2   AN ATTITUDE OF THE HEART

Geoffrey Bull, a British missionary to China who spent
years in Communist prisons, captured the essence of discipleship in his book, *When Iron Gates Yield*: "Discipleship is not therefore a state of being, but an attitude of
the heart toward the mind of Christ."[6] These words clearly

echo Psalms 119:111–112. In short, a true disciple wants
to know the Lord and become like Him. He or she yearns
to know the truth and to walk in its light. Such a person
regards doing the will of God here on earth as the best
response to the unspeakable mercy of having been given
new life in Christ. What else should that new life be used
for but to serve the Heavenly Father, since it is a priceless
gift from His Son? As Romans 12:1-2 states, "I beseech
you therefore, brethren, by the mercies of God, that you
present your bodies a living sacrifice, holy, acceptable to
God, which is your reasonable service. And do not be conformed to this world, but be transformed by the renewing
of your mind, that you may prove what is that good and
acceptable and perfect will of God." Doing the Lord's will,
and not our own, is also the best preparation for dwelling
with God forever. As Amos 3:3 points out, "Can two walk
together, unless they are agreed?" Now is the best time to
agree with the Lord and to learn His ways, dying to ourselves in the process.

How does this compare with the vision of the Christian life often depicted in our day, especially in the various
forms of prosperity teaching? Is it really true that we can
have Jesus *and* whatever else we want? Is new life in Christ
mainly about *us*—our happiness, our success, and our ma-
terial well-being? How can the eternal truths of the Gospel
find full expression within such narrow expectations? And
are some of us who are in positions to teach or preach to
others trying to proclaim a more palatable Gospel? Or are
we reminding sinners that following Jesus will ultimately
cost them everything? "When He had called the people to
*Himself* ... He said to them, 'Whoever desires to come after Me, let him deny himself, and take up his cross, and fol-

low Me.'" (Mark 8:34) Are we seeking *self-fulfillment*—as the world does—or are we seeking the fulfillment of God's purposes, as in Matthew 6:10: "Your kingdom come, Your will be done on earth as it is in heaven"?

In the 1980s, I heard a message given to Christian undergraduates at Yale University by an experienced missionary to the Middle East. He declared that the will of God is only for some believers—that those who do His will are generally going to suffer. He asked the students if this was what they really wanted in life. He then stated that the rest of us, those for whom God has no specific plans, should just try to be the best Christians we can, enjoying life wherever it takes us. This is a misleading statement, however. God has purposes for every believer, though not all may be willing to accept God's will for their life. And if doing the will of God involves suffering, as it may well, we are promised in Scripture that such suffering will bear fruit that will never pass away. Above all, remember 1 John 2:17, "the world is passing away, and the lust of it; but he who does the will of God abides forever." Should we who are believers therefore spend our lives doing our own thing, or should we do the will of God as lifelong disciples of Jesus?

How often do we Christians talk about laying down our lives for Jesus, as He laid down His life for us? Do we speak about suffering for Christ, about denying ourselves, taking up our cross, and living for God alone? Do we remind ourselves that we need to pray, as Jesus did, "Not my will, but Thine be done"? Many nineteenth-century Christians, like the English Puritans before them, viewed the building of godly *character* as one of their greatest pursuits in life. They labored at becoming *like* Christ more than on building a career or even a ministry. Becoming like Jesus is no easy task, as the great nineteenth-century English preacher, Charles Spurgeon, pointed out:

> Are you asking the reason for your trials, believer? Look *upward* to your heavenly Father, and behold Him pure and holy. Do you know that you are one day to be like Him? Will you easily be conformed to His image? Will you not require much refining in the *"furnace of affliction"* (Isa. 48:10) to purify you? Will it be an easy thing to get rid of your corruption and make you perfect, *"even as your Father which is in heaven is perfect"*? (Matthew 5:48)[7]

Along with forming godly character, Christians in every century who have desired to be disciples of Jesus have regarded walking in daily *communion* with Him as their first priority. As Jesus said in John 15:5, "He who abides in Me, and I in him, bears much fruit; *for without Me you can do nothing.*"

Yet do we truly believe what Jesus said? Do we understand that abiding in Christ is our greatest work in life, that He is the fountain from which every good and eternal fruit flows? Can we declare together with the apostle Paul,

> But what things were gain to me, these I have counted loss for Christ. Yet indeed I also count all things loss for the excellence of the knowledge of Christ Jesus my Lord, for whom I have suffered the loss of all things, and count them as rubbish, that I may gain Christ and be found in Him, not having my

own righteousness, which is from the law, but
that which is through faith in Christ, the righteousness which is from God by faith; *that I
may know Him* and the power of His resurrection, and the fellowship of His sufferings, being conformed to His death, if, by any means,
I may attain to the resurrection from the dead.
(Philippians 3:7–11, emphasis added)

Wait a minute! What is Paul so concerned about here?
We are all born-again believers, so we already know Jesus,
right? Besides, Christians in affluent countries rarely suffer
"the loss of all things." That happens mostly to unfortunate
believers in third world countries. We are doubly blessed
in that we get to have Jesus *and* our prosperity, too!

Besides, who is concerned in our day about *attaining*
"to the resurrection from the dead"? We are already saved,
so why would there be any question about *our* taking part
in the resurrection from the dead? And as for those believers who do suffer, if they had a little more sense and less fa-
naticism, they could easily avoid the trouble. At a ministe-
rial gathering I attended a few years ago, a man from India
declared that Christians in his country who are persecuted
for trying to reach the lost suffer because they are unwise
in their methods. With better techniques—and a deeper
appreciation of where unbelievers are coming from—they
could spare themselves such difficulties!

Some believers may in fact be unwise in their methods,
but then there are those like a former Hindu high priest
whom I met recently in New York City. Since his conver-
sion through a vision of Christ he received while serving in

a Hindu temple in southeast India, he has led tens of thousands of Hindus to faith in Jesus. His reward for his labors? He has had both of his wrists broken multiple times, his spine was broken as a result of a beating, and he was left for dead after being stoned. On top of that, he was put on public trial for converting Hindus to Christianity, ultimately having to flee his native land to escape from those who were out to kill him. His wife and young daughters had to live in hiding for another year and a half before they were able to escape and rejoin him in New York.

Have we missed something here? Are we so busy living in safe, shallow waters that we do not hear even God Himself calling us out into the Deep? As Hebrews 13:13 states, "Therefore let us go forth to Him, outside the camp, bearing His reproach." Written more than one hundred years ago, the words of A.B. Simpson's hymn, *Launch Out*, are prophetic regarding our generation:

> But many, alas! Only stand on the shore
> And gaze on the ocean so wide;
> They never have ventured
>     its depths to explore,
> Or to launch on the fathomless tide.
>
> Launch out into the deep,
> Oh let the shoreline go;
> Launch out, launch out in the ocean divine,
> Out where the full tides flow.[8]

Did Jesus stay safely by the shore? Did He try to avoid the trouble, or use a better technique to save us than a bloody cross? Did He seek to escape persecution? Or did

He launch out into the tides of a dangerous, rebellious world—leaving the safety of Heaven behind to rescue us from eternal destruction?

## 1.3   THE CROSS OF CHRIST

Charles H. Spurgeon wrote about the reality and purpose of suffering in the Christian life. His words are worth considering as he compares Christians to Simon the Cyrenian, the man whom the Romans compelled to bear Jesus' cross on the road to Golgotha:

> We see in Simon carrying the cross a picture of the work of the church throughout all generations; she is the cross-bearer for Jesus. Mark, then, Christian: Jesus does not suffer so as to exclude your suffering. He bears a cross, not that you may escape it, but that you may endure it. Christ exempts you from sin, but not from sorrow. Remember that, and expect to suffer. But let us comfort ourselves with this thought: that in our case, as in Simon's, it is not our cross, but Christ's cross that we carry.[9]

Thomas Shepherd also speaks of the need for every believer to bear the cross in one of his famous seventeenth-century hymns,

> Must Jesus bear the cross alone,
> And all the world go free?
> No, there's a cross for ev-'ry one,
> And there's a cross for me.[10]

The cross is not a convenient reality as it speaks of death, but it is an absolutely necessary one. In order to truly live, we must first reckon ourselves dead to sin, to our old ways of life, and to this fallen world. It is only as we die to self and are crucified with Christ that we realize the full power of Jesus' words in John 8:36, "if the Son makes you free, you shall be free indeed."

In fact, those who receive Jesus will indeed be set free, free from the awful power and domination of sin! But do we remember that the purpose of our newfound freedom is to serve the Lord, not our own lusts and desires? As Paul wrote in 1 Corinthians 6:19–20, "Or do you not know that your body is the temple of the Holy Spirit who is in you, whom you have from God, and *you are not your own*? For you were bought at a price; therefore glorify God in your body and in your spirit, *which are God's*."

Let us also consider the words of Isaac Watts' great eighteenth-century hymn, "Am I a Soldier of the Cross?" Who of us can sing this hymn without being convicted of how far short we fall respecting God's high calling in Christ Jesus?

> Am I a soldier of the cross,
> A follower of the Lamb,
> And shall I fear to own His cause,
> Or blush to speak His Name?
>
> Must I be carried to the skies
> On flowery beds of ease,
> While others fought to win the prize,
> And sailed through bloody seas?

Are there no foes for me to face?
Must I not stem the flood?
Is this vile world a friend to grace,
To help me on to God?

Sure I must fight if I would reign;
Increase my courage, Lord.
I'll bear the toil, endure the pain,
Supported by Thy Word.[11]

I well remember singing this anointed hymn during my childhood in a small-town New England Congregational church. God used its powerful message repeatedly to remind me of His higher calling on my life, something I at times very much wanted to escape. Should I seek to be carried to Heaven "on flowery beds of ease" while others around the globe suffer torments for the sake of Christ? I recently heard about American Christians who wrote to a minister in China. They told him that they were praying for him, that God would deliver him and his church from persecution. This Chinese servant of Christ wrote back that he was praying for them in America as well—that God would allow them to face persecution!

How could he write this? Because he knew from experience that persecution has a way of clarifying matters. It divides between the "wheat" and the "chaff." One day, when a dear friend teaching in China was feeling especially sorry for believers there because of all they suffer, a young Chinese Christian walked up to him and said, "I feel so sorry for you American Christians." In shock, my friend asked him what he meant, and he replied, "You think you can have Jesus *and* everything else. For us in China, following Jesus means losing everything, so we know the true value of having Him." My friend was surprised by the young student's words, but learned a valuable lesson that day.

How many Christians are trying to "have it all," while also seeking to follow Jesus? How many are trying to be a friend to "this vile world," even while hoping to be the Lord's friend? How often are success and affluence preached in churches—instead of the necessity of *letting go of our life on earth*, in order to gain the life that will last forever? As Jim Elliot, a missionary to the Waodani (or Auca) people of Ecuador, wrote in his journal on October 28, 1949, "One of the great blessings of heaven is the appreciation of heaven on earth ... . He is no fool who gives what he cannot keep to gain that which he cannot lose."[12] On January 8, 1956, pierced by the spears of those to whom he was bringing the Gospel, he laid down his life.

Are you trying to hold on to your life? Or are you willing to let it go—placing it in the faithful hands of Jesus?

## 1.4   CALLED TO BE DISCIPLES

The truth is that the Lord has plans for *every* life yielded to Him. He desires *all* of His children to enter into lifelong discipleship. In the timeless words of 1 John 2:15–17,

> Do not love the world or the things in the world. If anyone loves the world, the love of the Father is not in him. For all that is in the world—the lust of the flesh, the lust of the eyes, and the pride of life—is not of the Father

> but is of the world. And the world is passing
> away, and the lust of it; *but he who does the will*
> *of God abides forever.* (emphasis added)

Fallen human nature will always seek its happiness in
things here and now—and be disappointed. But should
we, having been redeemed from this world by Jesus, continue to seek our happiness in things that will pass away?
Should we live chiefly for ourselves—knowing that Christ
gave His all *for us*? Should it not be our joy to do the will
of our Heavenly Father, to please Him at all costs and fulfill His purposes for our lives? Proverbs 11:24–25 declares,
"There is one who scatters, yet increases more; and there
is one who withholds more than is right, but it leads to
poverty. *The generous soul will be made rich, and he who wa-*
*ters will also be watered himself.*" As a dear missionary friend
used to say, "You can never outgive God!" The more freely
we offer ourselves to Him, the more He will make us rich
channels of blessing for others.

There is a powerful and moving story behind the writ-
ing of a famous hymn from the nineteenth century. George
Matheson was a brilliant scholar who graduated with honors from Glasgow University in 1861. Yet during his studies, he became completely blind. Afterwards, he believed
that the Lord wanted him to go into the ministry, so he
spent four more years in theological studies. A devoted sis-
ter mastered Greek, Latin, and Hebrew—all so that she
could become her blind brother's lifelong helper, first in
his studies and later in ministry.

Yet when Matheson sought a pulpit after graduation,
the larger churches of Scotland made it clear that they
did not want a blind minister, no matter how brilliant. He

therefore took up a post at a small church in Innellan, a seaport and summer resort where he remained for eighteen years. It has also been said that he hoped to marry a particular young woman, but was turned down by her, again due to his blindness. Matheson was a man who suffered many bitter setbacks in life, yet he overcame them all by the grace of God. He preached with such anointing and brokenness that, in time, people traveled from all over Europe to hear him speak in that little Scottish church. The Lord made him "broken bread" and "poured out wine" for throngs of needy and hurting souls.

In the summer of 1882, during a time of great difficulty, he composed his most famous hymn. In his own words,

> It was composed with extreme rapidity; it seemed to me that its construction occupied only a few minutes, and I felt myself rather in the position of one who was being dictated to than an original artist. I was suffering from extreme mental distress, and the hymn was the fruit of pain... [13]

This hymn has blessed and encouraged multitudes of Jesus' followers ever since. It tells of the Lord's total claim upon our lives, as well as of the high cost of discipleship. The hymn also speaks of the death-life into which every servant of the Lord must enter—if he or she would experience the fruitfulness that God so greatly desires. There in his small rural parish in Innellan, Matheson wrote,

> O Love that wilt not let me go,
> I rest my weary soul in Thee;
> I give Thee back the life I owe,

That in Thine ocean depths it flow
May richer, fuller be.

O Light that followest all my way,
I yield my flickering torch to Thee;
My heart restores its borrowed ray,
That in Thy sunshine's blaze its day
May brighter, fairer be.

O Joy that seekest me through pain,
I cannot close my heart to Thee;
I trace the rainbow through the rain,
And feel the promise is not vain
That morn shall tearless be.

O Cross that liftest up my head,
I dare not ask to fly from Thee;
I lay in dust life's glory dead,
And from the ground there blossoms red
Life that shall endless be.[14]

Is Jesus speaking to you as you read these words? Is He ask-
ing you to give back to Him your life's "borrowed ray," so
that in His radiant sunshine, "its day may brighter, fairer
be?" Is the Lord calling you to let go of the things you
glory in most—your talents, your dreams, your posses-
sions, and even your life itself? If you hear His voice, don't
turn Him away! Respond quickly, "Yes, Lord," and He will
bring marvelous, eternal fruit out of a life that will otherwise be but "a vapor that appears for a little time and then
vanishes away." (James 4:14)

# 2 *The Biblical Church*

At this point, some historical perspective may help us grasp the larger picture of what it means to be a disciple. Since the ultimate purpose of discipleship is to take our place as living stones in God's eternal house, we need first to recognize what a great privilege it is to be members of Jesus' church. The Biblical church is described as His Body—and His Bride. In King David's words, "But who am I, and who are my people, that we should be able to offer so willingly as this? For all things come from You, and of Your own we have given You." (1 Chronicles 29:14) Like well-loved children who cannot fathom the sacrifices their parents have made, we take for granted truths and blessings passed on to us by others at great cost to themselves. Scriptural truths may seem obvious and accessible to us today, yet we fail to understand them deeply—or to realize how priceless they are. Most of us are also unaware of the history of fierce opposition to truth over centuries and even millennia.

## 2.1 Eternal temple, beloved bride

Like Matheson, many saints suffered greatly to gain spiritual understanding that we take for granted. They endured deprivation, persecution, imprisonment, and even death, to obtain what is so readily available to us. We will never fully appreciate what we have received, *nor take full hold of all that God has for us*, until we understand what the Biblical church is and why it has been so greatly contested over the last two thousand years. That church is no less than the eternal temple in which God Himself will dwell forever. As the Apostle Paul wrote in Ephesians 2:19–22,

> Now, therefore, you are no longer strangers and foreigners, but fellow citizens with the saints and members of the household of God, having been built on the foundation of the apostles and prophets, Jesus Christ Himself being the chief cornerstone, in whom the whole building, being fitted together, grows into a holy temple in the Lord, in whom you also are being built together for a dwelling place of God in the Spirit.

The church is also the beloved Bride that the Father has been preparing for His Son from the foundation of the world. It is described as the new Jerusalem in Revelation 21:2 (NIV), "I saw the Holy City, the new Jerusalem, coming down out of heaven from God, prepared as a bride beautifully dressed for her husband." We need to understand the New Testament pattern for the church, and its history, in order to comprehend more clearly God's high calling on those He sanctifies for His own purposes.

As Paul wrote to the Ephesians, Jew and Gentile are to be made one in the church, "fellow heirs, of the same body, and partakers of His promise in Christ through the

gospel." (Ephesians 3:6) As an apostle to the Gentiles
who had been given supernatural revelation regarding the
church, Paul desired

> ...to make all see what is the fellowship of
> the mystery, which from the beginning of the
> ages has been hidden in God who created
> all things through Jesus Christ; to the intent
> that now the manifold wisdom of God might
> be made known by the church to the prin-
> cipalities and powers in the heavenly places,
> according to the eternal purpose which He
> accomplished in Christ Jesus our Lord... .
> (Ephesians 3:9–11)

Is it any wonder that those evil principalities and powers
hate the church so much, given that "now the manifold
wisdom of God might be made known" to them "*by the
church*"? Truly when we, the congregation of the Lord, are
what we ought to be, "we are to God the fragrance of Christ
among those who are being saved and among those who
are perishing. To the one we are the aroma of death leading to death, and to the other the aroma of life leading to
life." (2 Corinthians 2:15–16)

The New Testament church began as assemblies of
Jewish and Gentile believers meeting together in various
cities. Members were born again, baptized in water, and
filled with the Spirit as well as with a fiery zeal for God.
Their leaders were servants of the local churches, not masters over them, and the members of those churches served
in a rich variety of ministries and giftings. They were part
of one holy family, each called to lay down their lives for

the sake of others, living for Christ and not for worldly
ambition. The holiness and purity of God's people was respected even among unbelievers, and the proclamation of
the Gospel was regularly accompanied by healings and the
working of remarkable miracles (Acts 5:12–16). (We will
talk extensively about the nature and pattern of the New
Testament Church later in this book—for there is much
more that needs to be said.)

## 2.2   OPPOSITION

Nevertheless, the purity, power, and unity of the Biblical
church came under heavy attack early on, both from without and within. Sadly, believers did not always overcome
assaults upon their sanctity, as well as upon their grasp of
truth. Paul was compelled to write to the church in Galatia, "I marvel that you are turning away so soon from Him
who called you in the grace of Christ, to a different gospel,
which is not another; but there are some who trouble you
and want to pervert the gospel of Christ. But even if we,
or an angel from heaven, preach any other gospel to you
than what we have preached to you, let him be accursed."
(Galatians 1:6–8)

We also know from Jesus' words to the churches of
Asia in Revelation 2 and 3 that such turning aside was
occurring in other places as well. Piece by piece, year
by year, false doctrine and tradition displaced spiritual
truth as human religious traditions were exalted in place
of Scriptural standards. Eternal truths were lost through
unfaithfulness and compromise, as well as through the
work of false teachings and false teachers. Those who proclaimed a mixed or false "gospel" persecuted and even

expelled those who held to the truth, as was the case with Diotrephes described in 3 John 9–10. The end result was that, within a few centuries after Christ's death, the original Gospel had been almost entirely supplanted by a "form of godliness" that denied the convicting, transforming work of the Holy Spirit. The living organism of the Body of Christ was almost entirely replaced by religious institutions whose leaders (*clergy*) claimed to be the guardians of truth—even as they removed the Word of God from the hands of the common people (the *laity*). Those few believers who still sought to live by the teachings of the New Testament became targets of slander, persecution, exile, imprisonment, and death. (Much of this history has been thoroughly documented by E.H. Broadbent in *The Pilgrim Church*.)

For about a thousand years, Christians had little or no access to the Bible, unless they were members of the hierarchies of religious organizations that claimed absolute authority over all of Christendom. Yet even these clerics were largely ignorant of the Scriptures. The Word of God was as absent among Gentile Christians as it was at times among the Jews in Old Testament days. As Amos 8:11 states,

> "Behold, the days are coming,"
>     says the Lord God,
> "that I will send a famine on the land,
>   not a famine of bread,
>   nor a thirst for water,
>   but of hearing the words of the LORD."

For centuries, there was strong resistance to the translation of the Bible into the languages of the common people.

Nevertheless, one by one, godly men arose in Europe who began the work of giving God's Word back to the masses. One of these was William Tyndale who in 1526 gave England its first printed New Testament, translated directly from the Greek. Later, he also translated the first 14 books of the Old Testament from Hebrew. Much of his work was incorporated into the *King James Version* of 1611, though some of his wording was altered to please religious officials of the day.

Tyndale was a Catholic priest who strongly believed that the way to God was through His Word. Therefore, the common people needed access to the Bible in their own language. This view brought him into conflict with church authorities, as can be seen in his conversation with a fellow clergyman he met in his travels:

> Not long after, Master Tyndale happened to be in the company of a certain divine, recounted for a learned man, and, in communing and disputing with him, he drove him to that issue, that the said great doctor burst out into these blasphemous words, "We were better to be without God's laws than the pope's." Master Tyndale, hearing this, full of godly zeal, and not bearing that blasphemous saying, replied, "I defy the pope, and all his laws;" and added, "If God spared him life, ere many years *he would cause a boy that driveth the plough to know more of the Scripture than he did.*"[1] (Emphasis added)

Tyndale later wrote of his work, "And now, because the lay and unlearned people are taught these first principles of our profession, therefore they read the scripture, and understand and delight therein."[2] Yet in 1536 this brave man paid with his life, executed by strangulation and then burning. While his executioner fastened him to a post, he cried out one last prayer on Henry VIII's behalf: "Lord, open the king of England's eyes!" This same king later authorized the sale of Tyndale's translation of the Bible throughout his kingdom—*fulfilling Tyndale's prophecy regarding English ploughboys.*[3]

## 2.3   RESTORATION

Over the last six hundred years or so, the common people have regained access to the Bible through the labors of faithful men and women like Tyndale. Through their work, the Lord has been restoring truths that had been buried for more than a millennium. These eternal truths include salvation by faith and not by works, the assurance of the forgiveness of sins, sanctification, holiness, the baptism of believers by immersion, and the baptism and gifts of the Holy Spirit. We today are the beneficiaries of the prayers and labors of many faithful believers in centuries past. These men and women stayed true to the Lord in the face of strong opposition, *often in circumstances where spiritual falsehood was far more prevalent than truth.* Yet, as Hebrews 11:39–40 states, "And all these, having obtained a good testimony through faith, did not receive the promise, God having provided something better for us, that they should not be made perfect apart from us."

Do we understand the value of what we have received, our inheritance together with all the saints—past, present, and future? Do we *really* understand? Or do we esteem

Biblical truths and promises too lightly, not realizing how costly they are?

We live in a time when the Lord is restoring to His church all of her New Testament fullness, so we need to understand what He is doing. The authentic church is not a human institution with fancy buildings, robes, and traditions, nor is it the fruit of comparative theology or human religious strategies. As John pointed out in chapter 1 of his Gospel, verses 12 and 13, "But as many as received Him, to them He gave the right to become children of God, to those who believe in His name: who were born, not of blood, nor of the will of the flesh, nor of the will of man, but of God." The church of Jesus Christ is a living assembly of "faithful ones" born again through the work of the Holy Spirit in order to serve the Lord for all their lives. They are "members of His body, of His flesh, and of His bones" (Ephesians 5:30), worshipping the Lord not according to human traditions, but "in spirit and truth." (John 4:23)

To understand what God is doing in our time, we must set aside centuries of tradition, including many things written by even the early church fathers in the second century AD and after. The teachings of the Bible have been buried under multiple layers of what people have taught and written over the last 1900 years. As is true of the Talmud, a collection of centuries of Jewish rabbinical commentary on the Scriptures, some writings are of real value—while others plainly contradict the Word of God. In Jesus' own words from Matthew 15:6 about rabbinical teachings in His day, "Thus you have made the commandment of God of no effect by your tradition." Yet are we Gentile Christians in a position to boast? Might not Jesus also say of some of us, with all our divisions and differences of opinion about doctrine and theology, "All too well you reject the commandment of God, that you may keep your tradition"? (Mark 7:9)

# 3   *False Prophets*

In examining what it means to be followers of Jesus and learning the truth about the Biblical church, we encounter another great danger besides replacing the Word of God with traditions. The Bible plainly warns us that there will also be false prophets in our day just as there were in Old Testament times. In fact, some of what we now call "tradition" actually began as the teachings of false prophets. Any careful scholar of the Scriptures will quickly realize that false prophets regularly outnumber true ones. Jesus Himself cautions us in Matthew 7:15–20,

> Beware of false prophets, who come to you in sheep's clothing, but inwardly they are ravenous wolves. You will know them by their fruits. Do men gather grapes from thornbushes or figs from thistles? Even so, every good tree bears good fruit, but a bad tree bears bad fruit…Therefore by their fruits you will know them.

If a man or woman claims to teach truth, yet contradicts God's Word or leads people into sin, that person is a deceiver and a false prophet. Even the seeming or actual ability to perform miracles is no guarantee that a person is genuinely of God. In Matthew 24:24, Jesus declares, "For false christs and false prophets will rise and show great signs and wonders to deceive, if possible, even the elect."

## 3.1  ACCORDING TO THEIR DESIRES

Here we need to honestly ask ourselves, what is it that we are seeking? Are we looking for signs and wonders, or are we yearning to know the living God? If we follow the Lord with all our hearts, we *will* see signs and wonders. But if we seek signs and spiritual experiences first, we may well get what we are looking for—and be led away from the truth! People do go astray, running after wonder merchants, especially when those merchants promise people what they already desire. As Oswald Chambers declared almost 100 years ago,

> So long as our wits and human solutions are on the throne, to satisfy the need of men is ostensibly the grandest thing to do. Every temptation of Satan will certainly seem right to us unless we have the Spirit of God. Fellowship with the Lord is the only way to detect them as being wrong.[1]

A while ago, I was in a staff prayer meeting at a prominent New York church and heard the pastor describe a conversation with a popular minister. He asked the man why his church was always so full of people. The man responded, "Because I tell them just what they want to hear." At least he was honest! But is this the kind of minister the church needs today, someone who helps fulfill 2 Timothy 4:3–4?

"For the time will come when they will not endure sound doctrine, but *according to their own desires*, because they have itching ears, they will heap up for themselves teachers; and they will turn their ears away from the truth, and be turned aside to fables."

When it comes to miracles, healings, and even genuine needs, we must remember the great Scriptural principle from Matthew 6:33, "But seek first the kingdom of God and His righteousness, and all these things shall be added to you." The Lord is God and He will not give His glory to another. He will not play second fiddle to anyone or anything. Even when our needs are indisputable and we are seeking the Lord for answers that come only from Him, we like Job must be willing to declare sincerely in the face of our troubles, "Though He slay me, yet will I trust Him." (Job 13:15) *What is it that we are seeking?* Is God Himself the goal of our lives—or, as Oswald Chambers put it, "is our goal something less, no matter how noble?"[2] Remember the words the Lord spoke to Abraham, the father of faith, nearly four thousand years ago: "Do not be afraid, Abram. I am your shield, your exceedingly great reward." (Genesis 15:1) *Any other reward is just too small!* But many do settle for far less than God Himself.

One of the most fearful warnings regarding the nature and work of false prophets is found in 2 Peter 2:1–3,

> But there were also false prophets among the people, even as there will be false teachers among you, who will secretly bring in destructive heresies, even denying the Lord who bought them, and bring on themselves swift

destruction. And many will follow their destructive ways, because of whom the way of
truth will be blasphemed. By covetousness
they will exploit you with deceptive words;
for a long time their judgment has not been
idle, and their destruction does not slumber.

Note first that Peter is saying that these false prophets will
be "among you." More than that, some of them will also be
people who were saved out of sin by the Lord, but they fail
to hold fast to the truth. As Paul warned the Ephesian elders in Acts 20:29–30, "For I know this, that after my de-
parture savage wolves will come in among you, not sparing the flock. Also *from among yourselves* men will rise up,
speaking perverse things, to draw away the disciples after
themselves." (Emphasis added)

Here we find one of the keys to the true nature of false
prophets—their aim is to build their own little kingdoms
while they claim to build the church of Jesus Christ. Just
as in detective work, *it all comes down to motive*! No wonder Paul warned Timothy, "Watch your life and doctrine
closely. Persevere in them, because if you do, you will save
both yourself and your hearers." (1 Timothy 4:16, NIV)
Consider the alternative, losing your own soul and leading astray those to whom you minister! When believers
are careless about their lives and beliefs, the love of things
and of pleasure soon replaces the love of God. Sin, deception, and covetousness quickly follow on the coattails of
the love of "this present world," as was the case with De-
mas described in 2 Timothy 4:10.

Peter echoes Paul's words when he writes of false
prophets, "By covetousness they will exploit you with de-

ceptive words..." How often the Bible warns us against covetousness! The human heart is quickly drawn away from the love of God by the love of things. No wonder John wrote in 1 John 2:15, "Do not love the world or the things in the world. If anyone loves the world, the love of the Father is not in him...." Colossians 3:5 connects covetousness or greed directly with idolatry, the worship of other gods. Like the false prophets of old, modern false prophets lead people astray from the worship of the One True God by "deceptive words" and false promises. As 2 Peter 2:18-19 states,

> ...they mouth empty, boastful words and, by appealing to the lustful desires of sinful human nature, they entice people who are just escaping from those who live in error. They promise them freedom, while they themselves are slaves of depravity—for a man is a slave to whatever has mastered him. (NIV)

Sadly, not only do their false teachings lead people astray, but their work causes the church itself to be spoken against. As Jude 4 declares, these are "ungodly men, who turn the grace of our God into lewdness and deny the only Lord God and our Lord Jesus Christ." And again from Jude 12, "These are spots in your love feasts, while they feast with you without fear, serving only themselves."

## 3.2   TWICE DEAD

If the fragrance of Christ and the fruit of the Spirit in the lives of the saints can cause even an unbelieving world to honor God, what a devilish work it is when the stench of immorality and worldliness defiles those who were once clothed in white. As the prophet Nathan stated in his reproof of David after he committed adultery with Bathsheba, "by doing this you have made the enemies of the LORD show utter contempt." (2 Samuel 12:14, NIV) Contempt of whom but of God Himself?

Do our actions as those who bear the name of Christ cause the world to fear and honor God? Or do we provoke unbelievers to blaspheme the Lord who bought us, because of our hypocrisy? Hypocrisy is a strong word, but it is used many times in the New Testament. It comes from the Greek *hupŏkrisis* (ὑπόκρισις), "acting under a feigned part," as with an actor on a stage assuming the character of another.[3] Are we real with God and men, or are we pretending to be something we are not? This may seem like a simple question, but it is actually profound.

False prophets do not generally start out aiming to be false, yet at some point they begin to pretend to be something they are not. This is why "hypocrisy" is so frequently used as a description of those who are false: "Now the Spirit expressly says that in latter times some will depart from the faith, giving heed to deceiving spirits and doctrines of demons, speaking lies in hypocrisy, having their own conscience seared with a hot iron... ." (1 Timothy 4:1–2) It should be noted here that it is clear from the Greek that it is the demons who speak "lies in hypocrisy," feeding those lies into the minds of those who "depart from the faith." When a follower of Jesus sins, there are two choices. Either we confess our sin and repent of it, renouncing the work of the deceiving spirits who led us into error and returning to the way of truth. Or we refuse to confess and forsake our sin, effectively defending the work of the evil spirits who led us astray. Those who choose to do the latter rarely remain honest for long about their true spiritual condition—especially since sin itself *is* deception. And where there is deception, hypocrisy will soon follow. "If therefore the light that is in you is darkness, how great is that darkness!" (Matthew 6:23)

Jude 12–13 states of these false brethren and the disgrace they bring into the congregation of the saints,

> These are spots in your love feasts, while they feast with you without fear, *serving only themselves.* They are clouds without water, carried about by the winds; late autumn trees without fruit, twice dead, pulled up by the roots; raging waves of the sea, foaming up their own shame; wandering stars for whom is reserved the blackness of darkness forever. (Emphasis added)

By contrast, Paul wrote of love in 1 Corinthians 13:4–5, "Love suffers long and is kind; love does not envy; love does not parade itself, is not puffed up; does not behave rudely, *does not seek its own...*" May God grant us discernment to distinguish clearly between truth and falsehood, as well as between those who truly serve God and those who serve only themselves.

### 3.3   LORD, GRANT YIELDEDNESS

May the Lord also grant us grace to yield to Him all that we have and are so that no room is left for covetousness, idolatry, or hypocrisy. As David cried out in Psalm 86:11, "Teach me Your way, O LORD; I will walk in Your truth;

*Unite my heart to fear Your name."* For most of us, getting to the place of having a single heart towards God is a real battle. The most difficult day of my young life occurred when I was a freshman at Yale. I was sure that I was already wholeheartedly following the Lord, meeting for prayer six mornings a week, going to Bible studies twice a week, preaching in the open air on campus, and attending church on Sunday mornings. Yet, as a sophomore said to me one Saturday morning, "Chris, you are like a person with your feet in two different boats. One of your feet is in the boat of the Kingdom of Heaven, and the other is in the boat of this world. At some point, the boats are going to separate, and you will either have to make up your mind and put both feet in one of the boats, or you will be torn apart."

I did not like what my friend said to me, but I was so convicted by his words that I was absolutely miserable for the rest of the day. I felt exactly like Jonathan Edwards' famous spider dangling over the fires of hell ("The God that holds you over the pit of hell, much as one holds a spider…he looks upon you as worthy of nothing else, but to be cast into the fire… .")[4] God was making it plain that He was not going to take second place in my life: not to sports, not to friends, nor to anything else. Like those to whom Edwards was preaching, I knew the truth and, as a senior in high school, had even told the Lord that I would do His will. Now I had to decide once and for all to crown Jesus as King of *every* aspect of my life—with nothing held back!

After hours of torment, I did decide at about 1:15 AM Sunday morning. I yielded my pitiful all to God to do His will and not mine for the rest of my days. The terror and misery of that day evaporated instantly, and I fell asleep, waking up the next morning dancing and singing. *You see, we just have to make up our minds*! Will we let God be God, whatever it costs? Or will we hold onto the reins of our lives—and risk betraying the One who bought us with His precious blood?

# 4  *The Call of God*

> To Him who loved us and washed us from our
> sins in His own blood, and has made us *kings and
> priests* to His God and Father, to Him be glory
> and dominion forever and ever. Amen.

> Revelation 1:5–6

There is only one standard by which every teaching and
life should (and will) be judged, by comparing it to the
whole counsel of the Word of God. We must go back
to the source of all revealed truth, the Bible, and examine again what the Scriptures testify regarding the church.
In the New Testament church, God invites *all* believers
to become disciples. All are called to minister (serve) in
the church, *though in differing capacities.* As 1 Corinthians
12:27–31 states,

> Now you are the body of Christ, and *each
> one of you is a part of it.* And in the church
> God has appointed first of all apostles, sec-
> ond prophets, third teachers, then workers of
> miracles, also those having gifts of healing,
> those able to help others, those with gifts of

> administration, and those speaking in differ-
> ent kinds of tongues. Are all apostles? Are all
> prophets? Are all teachers? Do all work mira-
> cles? Do all have gifts of healing? Do all speak
> in tongues? Do all interpret? But eagerly de-
> sire the greater gifts. (NIV, emphasis added)

What a rich description of the varied functions of the
members of Christ's Body! We often read these words, *yet
do we really believe them*? If strangers were to enter among
us today, is this the reality that they would see—a multi-
plicity of ministries (*diakonia*, or practical service), spiritual gifts, and functions? Or would they see a congregation
of many waiting for one or even a few individuals to do the
work of the ministry?

Ephesians 4:11–13 provides us with another priceless
glimpse into God's plan for His church:

> And He Himself gave some to be apostles,
> some prophets, some evangelists, and some
> pastors and teachers, for the equipping of the
> saints for the work of ministry, for the edify-
> ing of the body of Christ, till we all come to
> the unity of the faith and of the knowledge of
> the Son of God, to a perfect man, to the mea-
> sure of the stature of the fullness of Christ....

Note here that even apostles, prophets, evangelists, pastors and teachers have as their *chief* purpose the preparation of *all* God's people to serve (minister to) the Lord.
Their job is not to build their own "ministries," but to pre-
pare an eternal house for the living God. Yet how often we
fall short of the Biblical pattern for that house! If the Lord

commanded Moses regarding the earthly temple, "And see to it that you make them according to the pattern which was shown you on the mountain" (Exodus 25:40), how much more careful should we be in building God's eternal temple—the Body of Christ?

## PRIESTS AND KINGS

Though the Lord separated the priests from the Levites in the Old Testament, and the Levites from the rest of the people, it is plain in Scripture that there is no longer to be a *separate* priestly caste in the New Testament church. Revelation 1:5-6 states that we are *all* called to be kings and priests unto our God. The Greek word translated here as "kings" is *basilĕían* (βασιλείαν, bas-i-leí-an, royalty or a kingdom).[1] It is the singular objective case form of *basilĕía*, a word that appears frequently in the New Testament in phrases like the "kingdom" (*basilĕía*) of heaven. It is also clear from our Savior's words in Luke 22:25–27, that there are to be no "lords of the church" other than the One Lord,

> The kings (*basileís*, βασιλείς)[2] of the Gentiles exercise lordship over them, and those who exercise authority over them are called "benefactors." But not so among you; on the contrary, he who is greatest among you, let him be as the younger, and he who governs as he who serves. For who is greater, he who sits at the table, or he who serves? Is it not he who sits at the table? Yet I am among you as the One who serves.

This fallen world is all about self-fulfillment, selfish ambition, power, and domination. But the Kingdom of Heaven is about laying down our lives to serve the Lord *and* others. As Matthew 16:25–26 states, "For whoever desires to save his life will lose it, but whoever loses his life for My sake will find it. For what profit is it to a man if he gains the whole world, and loses his own soul? Or what will a man give in exchange for his soul?" By the way, the English words "life" and "soul" in this passage are translations of the exact same Greek word, *psucheén*.[3]

At a Bible study in college, a friend once asked, "What would you call a pillar surrounded by blocks of stone lying at its feet?" He waited a moment, and then answered his own question, "Ruins!" He pointed out that the purpose of a pillar is to hold up other stones over its head, to "exalt" other stones and not itself. And so it must be with those who are the *pillars* of the church of Jesus Christ. What a perfect illustration of Paul's words in Philippians 2:3–4, "Let nothing be done through selfish ambition or conceit, but in lowliness of mind *let each esteem others better than himself*. Let each of you look out not only for his own interests, but also for the interests of others." Some of us naturally desire to have others gather at our feet so that we may lead them, while others of us would rather let others do the leading, preferring to be followers. No matter what our personal preferences may be, however, we all must take up our cross and deny ourselves—if we are to truly build the church of Jesus, and not produce a pile of ruins! As 1 Corinthians 3:11–13 states, "For no other foundation can anyone lay than that which is laid, which is Jesus Christ. Now if anyone builds on this foundation with gold, silver, precious stones, wood, hay, straw, each one's work will become clear; for the Day will declare it, because it will be revealed by fire; and the fire will test each one's work, of what sort it is."

How then are we to reign as kings in this life? The *New International Version* contains a remarkable translation of Romans 5:17: "For if, by the trespass of the one man, death reigned through that one man, how much more will those who receive God's abundant provision of grace and of the gift of righteousness *reign in life through the one man, Jesus Christ.*" (Emphasis added) As Isaiah prophesied in 26:13 (NIV), "O LORD, our God, other lords besides you have ruled over us, but your name alone do we honor." All of us were once ruled by one form of sin or another, pushed about by lust, jealousy, envy, anger, and other inordinate emotions. Though we did not know it, we were prisoners of the evil one, "having been taken captive by him to do his will." (2 Timothy 2:26) We thought we were doing our *own* will, but we were deceived by the one who "would not let his captives go home." (Isaiah 14:17, NIV) Yet now we have received overflowing grace in Jesus Christ, and are clothed in a righteousness that we could never earn. Oh, that God would give us grace to see what a marvelous privilege we have! We have been set free to "reign in life" through Jesus, serving Him and others, rather than living under the oppression of sin, selfishness, and fear of death.

Not only are we called to be kings, we have also been called to be priests (ἱερείς or *hiereís*).[4] In the old covenant, the king could not become a priest and priests could not serve as king. The total divide between kings and priests continued until the true Priest/King, Jesus (Yeshua), came and laid down His life as an eternal sacrifice for sin on the cross. As Hebrews 2:17–18 states of our

Savior, "Therefore, in all things He had to be made like His brethren, that He might be a merciful and faithful High Priest in things pertaining to God, to make propitiation for the sins of the people. For in that He Himself has suffered, being tempted, He is able to aid those who are tempted." It is only through His redemption that we can now become both "kings and priests" unto our God.

What does it mean to be a priest? Like Jesus, our High Priest "who, in the days of his flesh…offered up prayers and supplications" (Hebrews 5:7), we are called to pray that our Father's purposes be accomplished in this fallen world. Prayer is the greatest, most powerful weapon in the believer's arsenal, yet how often this mighty instrument is used for defensive, and not offensive purposes. In the words of Oswald Chambers,

> Launch out in reckless belief that the Redemption is complete, and then bother no more about yourself, but begin to do as Jesus Christ said—pray for the friend who comes to you at midnight, pray for the saints, pray for all men….[5]

The heart of a true priest of God is not self-absorbed, *but taken up in the needs and cares of others.* And as priests, we are like Jesus to be separate from this world and holy unto God. "Depart! Depart! Go out from there, touch no unclean thing; go out from the midst of her, be clean, you who bear the vessels of the LORD." (Isaiah 52:11) What a marvelous calling we have to be priests and kings before

Almighty God, and what a privilege to be consecrated co-workers with Jesus in the work of rescuing souls out of a dying world.

# 5   Freedom or Bondage?

God's original purpose for the Jewish people was not that
they should have a human king, but that they should live
freely under the sovereign rule of their eternal King, the
Lord Himself. Micah 4:4–5 states,

> But everyone shall sit
> under his vine and under his fig tree,
> and no one shall make them afraid;
> For the mouth of the LORD of hosts
> has spoken.
>
> For all people walk
> each in the name of his god,
> But we will walk
> in the name of the LORD our God
> forever and ever.

Oh what freedom and power there is walking in "the name
of the LORD our God forever"! Yet the Jewish people lost
much of their personal liberty when they insisted on having a human king to rule over them, rather than their Heavenly King. This desire for a visible, human king, rather
than the invisible Lord, is strong in fallen human nature.

The Gentiles have proven to be no wiser in this than the children of Israel.

## 5.1   THE GREAT DIVIDE

The Biblical church of Jesus Christ has only one Lord, and all the members of His Body are called to liberty as brothers and sisters who are "members of one another." Nevertheless, as the early church went into decline, a great divide entered among the generality of Christians, that between what has come to be known as the *clergy* (ministers), and the *laity* (the people). It is worth noting that a term so widely used today as "clergy" has its earliest roots in a Greek word, kleros (κληρος, klaý-ros), which appears only a few times in the New Testament—with a far different meaning than the term connotes today. (A fuller explanation of the etymology may be found in the endnotes).[1]

The Greek word *kleros* was not a priest or clergyman in any sense of the term. It initially meant "a shard used in casting lots." This usage derives from the ancient practice of using bits of wood, or other items such as dice, for the purpose of drawing chances—as we see in the casting of lots by the Roman soldiers who crucified Jesus to decide who would win his garments (Matthew 27:35). What was obtained purely by chance became known over time as the portion (*kleros*) received. By historical extension, or later even by acquisition (purchase), the term referred to a heritage, inheritance, lot, or part. These are the meanings of the term we actually encounter in the New Testament. Other than in the Gospel accounts of the dividing of Jesus' garments by casting lots, *kleros* appears only in Acts 1:26 ("And they cast their *lots*, and the *lot* fell on Matthias. And

he was numbered with the eleven apostles."), and in Acts
8:21 ("You have neither part nor *portion* in this matter, for
your heart is not right in the sight of God.")[2]

In the Septuagint, the earliest Greek version of the Old
Testament, *kleros* appears about one hundred and forty
times, translating eight Hebrew words. Three of these refer to lots literally—one being the "pur" of Purim in the
book of Esther. Five refer to *inheritance,* the portion one
receives. *Kleros* appears frequently in Numbers, Deuteronomy, Joshua, Judges, and Esther, but not a single reference
makes use of the word to make a religious distinction.

The Latin term *clericus* (a priest) as well as the similar
Greek term *klerikos* (an adjective meaning "of the clergy"
in hierarchical church jargon) had their roots in the original Greek term *kleros.* However, by the time Jerome pro-
duced the fourth-century Latin Vulgate translation of the
Bible at the request of Pope Damasus,[3] *clericus* referred to
the body of men ordained to minister in the Church as
*separate* from the rest of the people who were to receive
ministry. This division between ministers and the people
is something that had become the rule within the Roman
Catholic Church, and it would continue to be the practice in the Eastern Orthodox churches after they broke
away from Rome in 1054. Some of the higher clergy in
the Roman church are even described as the "princes"
of the church. Ministries (positions of service) that had
once been appointed by the Holy Spirit began to be ap-
portioned by hierarchical authorities. In time, they even
began to be purchased through the payment of money (often called "simony," a reference to the actions of Simon the
sorcerer in Acts 8:21 who tried to *buy* from the apostles the
ability to baptize others in the Holy Spirit).

At various times in church history, positions of so-called ministry have even been viewed as patrimonies (inherited positions), or "livings," speaking more of the *income generated* than the *service provided*. Sons of aristocrats who could not make a living in the world at large obtained a "living" (salaried position) within the institutional church, with the help of others in places of influence. It mattered little whether they were fit to hold such positions, so this practice inevitably helped to bring about spiritual decline within what was then called the "church." Ironically, this idea of a position in the church as a "living" is reflected in the Greek word *kleros*, the portion or lot received. Tragically, reducing the idea of service in the New Testament church only to a means to obtain a "living" completely misses the point of what Biblical ministry is all about. As Jesus said in Luke 22:27, "I am among you as the One who serves," a passage we will examine further later.

At this point, it is instructive to note that there is a strong warning in the Bible about a doctrine already existing in New Testament days that would in time lead to the oppression of God's people. In Revelation 2:6 (NIV), the Bible warns about the teaching and practice of the *Nicolaitans* (Νικολαϊτῶν, Nikolaitôn)[4] : "But you have this in your favor: You hate the practices of the Nicolaitans, which I also hate." Revelation 2:15–16 (NIV) also states: "Likewise you also have those who hold to the teaching of the Nicolaitans. Repent therefore! Otherwise, I will soon come to you and will fight against them with the sword of my mouth." This word is often translated as "followers of Nicolas," but there is no historical evidence for this. The literal translation is "conquerors of the people" (*niko* or "conquer," and *laos* "people," plus a noun case ending).[5]

It would seem from the text that the *Nicolaitans* were literally people who brought division among God's people, setting up certain individuals in positions separate from and in authority over the rest of the congregation. The term *kleros*, transformed into *klericus* or *clergy*, was probably chosen as the term for this separate caste of ministers as an attempt to link themselves to the Levitical priesthood—as in 1 Chronicles 24:7–18, "Now the first *lot* fell to Jehoiarib, the second to Jedaiah, the third to Harim ... ," *lot* here being translated from *kleros* in the Septuagint.

## 5.2   LORDS OR SERVANTS?

This division between the ministers and the people is clearly what happened historically as the original New Testament pattern of the church was buried—an undivided congregation of the saints in direct communion with God. It was replaced by a hierarchical model in which the common people had to go through a priestly caste in order to obtain access to God—the common religious pattern even in the ancient world. Remember again what Jesus said in Luke 22:25–26, "The kings of the Gentiles exercise lordship over them, and those who exercise authority over them are called 'benefactors.' But not so among you; on the contrary, he who is greatest among you, let him be as the younger, and he who governs as he who serves." In the light of this statement, is it any wonder that the Lord *hates* (μισέω, or misĕō, a very strong word)[6] the practices of those who are "conquerors of the people," rather than their servants?

If as Jesus stated in John 8:36, "Therefore if the Son makes you free, you shall be free indeed," how incensed the Lord must be at those who would bring back into captivity the very ones whom He set free by His death on the cross. The idea of being a disciple, *a direct recipient of the grace of God*, and a direct follower of Jesus without need of a mediator in the form of a priest or a church hierarchy, was deliberately buried for centuries. Many were persecuted and killed over the last two millennia for insisting as 1 Timothy 2:5 states, "For there is one God and one Mediator between God and men, the Man Christ Jesus." Even today, many people *still* do not realize that they can have a direct relationship with the Heavenly Father through the Son.

The whole idea of the Christian church as a *hierarchy* (graded or ranked positions of authority one above another) is not Biblical, as may be seen by examining the Scriptures. In the early church, the model of leadership we encounter in the church is very different from the later traditions that supplanted it. The church as a whole as well as in local congregations was to have multiple "servers" acting in multiple capacities. Apostles, prophets, evangelists, pastors, and teachers are servants of the church, appointed by God. Note that they are always mentioned *in the plural* in Scripture—with good reason. As Proverbs 11:14 declares. "Where there is no counsel, the people fall; but in the multitude of counselors there is safety." "Counsel" is not the opinion of one, but the working together of many to reach wise conclusions.

Instead of just one or two men, the leadership in the local churches or congregations of the New Testament consisted of multiple *elders*, who were charged with the overall care of the local church, and *deacons* ("servers") who specifically handled the natural and financial concerns. Once again, leadership in the Body of Christ was to be plural, bringing a balance and a fullness that no one believer can ever have by him or herself. Unlike this world, the "number one" that the Lord is looking for is spiritual oneness and love among His people. If anyone had the right to "lord" it over others, it would have been Jesus, yet He came as a servant who laid down His life for God's people. In Philippians 2:5–8, Paul exalted Jesus as an example of how we also should behave,

> Let this mind be in you which was also in Christ Jesus, who, being in the form of God, did not consider it robbery to be equal with God, *but made Himself of no reputation*, taking the form of a bondservant, and coming in the likeness of men. And being found in appearance as a man, He humbled Himself and became obedient to the point of death, even the death of the cross. (Emphasis added)

What an unworldly concept this is, not to seek reputation, or fame, or power—but to be a servant of others! And that is exactly what the members of Christ's Body are called to do.

In a situation among His disciples where the ancient human desire to be number one had raised its ugly head, Jesus could not have responded more plainly,

> Now there was also a dispute among them, as to which of them should be considered the

> greatest. And He said to them, "The kings of
> the Gentiles exercise lordship over them, and
> those who exercise authority over them are
> called 'benefactors.' But not so among you; on
> the contrary, he who is greatest among you,
> let him be as the younger, and he who governs
> as he who serves. For who is greater, he who
> sits at the table, or he who serves? Is it not he
> who sits at the table? Yet I am among you as
> the One who serves." (Luke 22:24–27)

So then those who are charged with watching over and
leading Christ's church are not to behave like the "kings
of the Gentiles," exercising "lordship" and "authority" over
others "inferior" to themselves. Instead, they are to make
themselves *inferior* to others in the original sense of the
word, *behaving as one of lower rank*—exactly the position
of a true servant, not of a ruler!

Traditional hierarchies, in which ministers are separated out as *superior* to the common people, turn the Biblical model for the church on its head. Yet these traditional
forms predominate today. One reason that this happened
is because many of the great figures of Protestant history
were *Reformers*, not *Restorers*. Martin Luther was aiming
to *reform* the church, starting from the Catholic model he
knew so well—and thank God he did! The largest part of
his work has been a blessing to all of us ever since. Yet because he did not set out to *restore* God's house to its original New Testament pattern, he effectively passed on practices that have no basis in the Bible. Sadly, he even included
a strong dose of anti-Semitism in his later years. He re-
tained Catholic traditions such as one-man leadership in

the local church. Whether you call that person the priest or the pastor, it is a very different model from that of multiple elders watching over each local church. Consider again what Paul wrote to Titus in chapter 1, verse 5, "For this reason I left you in Crete, that you should set in order the things that are lacking, and appoint elders in every city as I commanded you." But we will look more at this matter later.

## 5.3  GOD'S WORD OR MAN'S OPINION?

The most critical issue here is whether eternal truth will prevail among God's people, or whether human opinion in all its variety will be allowed to displace that truth. As a dear servant of the Lord said years ago, "It does not matter who you are or how old you are in the Lord, if a child speaks the truth, we all should listen." By contrast, remember what the good Catholic doctor said to Tyndale, "We were better to be without God's laws than the pope's." That statement may seem shocking to us today yet, in one form or another, it has been repeated among Christians countless times ever since. Whenever we decide that the doctrines of our particular denomination or spiritual leader are *more important than the whole counsel of the Word of God*, we are essentially affirming just what the doctor said. As Paul reproved the church in Corinth,

> Now I plead with you, brethren, by the name of our Lord Jesus Christ, that you all speak the same thing, and that there be no divisions among you, but that you be perfectly joined together in the same mind and in the same

judgment. For it has been declared to me concerning you, my brethren, by those of Chloe's
household, that there are contentions among
you. Now I say this, that each of you, says, "I
am of Paul," or "I am of Apollos," or "I am of
Cephas," or "I am of Christ." Is Christ divided?
Was Paul crucified for you? Or were you baptized in the name of Paul? (1 Corinthians
1:10–13)

Years ago, I heard an evangelical minister declare that
1 Corinthians is a book for "baby Christians," one that no
member of *his* congregation need bother with. If that is in
fact so, then Christianity is filled with "baby Christians"
who absolutely *need* to read this book! The multitude of
divisions among believers today is simply one more good
reason why 1 Peter 4:17 declares that "the time has come
for judgment to begin at the house of God...." Believers will "all appear before the judgment seat of Christ,
that each one may receive the things done in the body...."
(2 Corinthians 5:10) We are treading in perilous waters
when we become followers of men, no matter what their
titles or positions, rather than followers of Jesus Himself.
The unchanging reality is that it is not title or position in
the church that matters, but whether each of us is right
with God, and whether we are "speaking the truth in love."
(Ephesians 4:15) *When position and title become more important than Biblical truth, God's people are in great danger.*

Jesus spoke plainly about this matter of titles in
Matthew 23:6–12, words that we would do well to heed.
Speaking of the scribes and Pharisees, He said,

> They love the best places at feasts, the best
> seats in the synagogues, greetings in the mar-
> ketplaces, and to be called by men, 'Rabbi,
> Rabbi.' But you, do not be called 'Rabbi';
> for One is your Teacher, the Christ, and you
> are all brethren. Do not call anyone on earth
> your father; for One is your Father, He who
> is in heaven. And do not be called teachers
> (*kathegetai*); For One is your Teacher, the
> Christ. But he who is greatest among you shall
> be your servant. And whoever exalts himself
> will be humbled, and he who humbles himself
> will be exalted.

Jesus' final words here are especially important. Behind
mankind's love affair with titles lies a great deal of pride.
Two people may be doing exactly the same work, but if one
of them has a more impressive title, that person may feel
much better about his or her position. Also, one does not
necessarily have to function in the New Testament sense
to be given a title; it may even serve as an extra-Biblical
shortcut to recognition.

Oh, how we love to be somebody! Yet the example we
are to follow is that of Jesus, "who, being in the form of
God ... made Himself of no reputation, taking the form of
a bondservant, and coming in the likeness of men. And
being found in appearance as a man, He humbled Himself and became obedient to the point of death, even the
death of the cross." (Philippians 2:6–8) The heart of the
Christian life is not about self-exaltation—that is what this
fallen world runs after. We are called to humble ourselves
as Jesus did, and to die to ourselves so that God can have

His way in our lives. And when He has His way in us, even then the glory will not go to us but to Him!

Replacing Scriptural leadership with religious hierarchy always costs believers their liberty under God. The Lord calls Christians to "reign in life," yet religious hierarchies have reigned over and oppressed Christians in one form or another for centuries. No wonder Paul warned in 1 Corinthians 7:23, "*You were bought at a price; do not become slaves of men.*" Paul was speaking first and foremost of physical slavery, but spiritual slavery is a great danger as well. It is true that some and even many religious officials genuinely do fear God. They do their best to advance God's kingdom as far as they understand it. But because, in an organizational setting, *the position eventually becomes more important than the man,* others come after them who are not so careful about truth. Ironically, this is exactly what happened with the kings of Judah. Godly kings were followed and outnumbered by ungodly kings—precisely because Gentile-style kingship was never what God intended for Israel. Israel already had a king—it was God Himself!

Remember also that Ephesians 4:14 warns us, "that we should no longer be children, tossed to and fro and carried about with every wind of doctrine, by the trickery of men, in the cunning craftiness of deceitful plotting...." The true ministries listed in verse 11 are given specifically for the preparation of God's people so that they should no longer be victims of false teachers and doctrines. Yet, if there were false prophets in Old Testament times, should we be surprised that there have also been false prophets in the years since? Were we not warned in 2 Peter 2:1–3?

But there were also false prophets among the

people, just as there will be false teachers
among you. They will secretly introduce destructive heresies, even denying the sovereign
Lord who bought them—bringing swift destruction on themselves. Many will follow
their shameful ways and will bring the way
of truth into disrepute. In their greed these
teachers will exploit you with stories they
have made up. Their condemnation has long
been hanging over them, and their destruction has not been sleeping. (NIV)

"In their greed" speaks of the all too frequent connection
between the love of money and the distortion of God's
Word. When either greed or sexual immorality reign in
the heart, false doctrine, exploitation of the saints, and the
corrupting of some who formerly walked in light soon fol-
lows.

No wonder the Lord has called us to be *disciples,*
student-followers of Himself and His Word! Every one of
us *must* know the Bible for our own sake as well as for the
sake of others. We need to be familiar with *every* aspect of
its message, so that we can discern between teachings that
truly are of God and those that have been twisted by men.
If we have been called to be kings, should not the Lord de-
mand of us at least as much as He demanded of the ancient
kings of Israel?

Also it shall be, when he sits on the throne of
his kingdom, that he shall write for himself a
copy of this law in a book, from the one before the priests, the Levites. And it shall be

> with him, and *he shall read it all the days of
> his life*, that he may learn to fear the LORD his
> God and be careful to observe all the words
> of this law and these statutes, *that his heart
> may not be lifted above his brethren*, that he
> may not turn aside from the commandment
> to the right hand or to the left, and that he may
> prolong his days in his kingdom, he and his
> children in the midst of Israel. (Deuteronomy
> 17:18–20, emphasis added)

Unfortunately, many Israelite kings failed to fulfill their
duty in this matter—with tragic consequences for themselves and for the Jewish people. Yet many believers do no
better when it comes to studying and knowing the Bible. In
Matthew 4:4, Jesus quoted from Deuteronomy, "Man shall
not live by bread alone, but by every word that proceeds
from the mouth of God." If the Word of God is indeed our
bread, no wonder so many of us are malnourished! The
Biblical church is an *organism*, not an *organization*—or
the property of any organization. The life and vitality of
that organism depends on how regularly *all* the people of
God feed upon God's Word. It also depends on each one
of us guarding our hearts against being "lifted above" our
brethren, and falling into the devil's own sin—pride.

## 5.4  WASHED IN THE BLOOD AND IN THE WORD

There is another reason why every follower of Jesus needs
to spend time daily studying the Bible, and it was a dear
Jewish friend who pointed it out to me. My wife and I recently attended a meeting in Manhattan where a Messianic

minister, Steve Fenchel, was giving one of a series of talks regarding the tabernacle of ancient Israel. He first pointed out that the Bible devotes a remarkably large amount of text to the plan of the tabernacle, right down to the smallest details. There is also an exacting description of the ministry and sacrifices that were to take place within it. Not only did the Lord lay out the pattern of the tabernacle with great care, but He also commanded Moses, "And see to it that you make them according to the pattern which was shown you on the mountain." (Exodus 25:40)

Why was it so important that the tabernacle be made exactly according to heavenly specifications? This Jewish minister explained that, among other things, the structure and function of the tabernacle are actually prophetic of the new covenant God would later bring about through Jesus, the Messiah. Specifically, he pointed out that there were two large objects that were to be placed in the courtyard of the Tabernacle. The first, which was closer to the outside entrance to the courtyard, was the bronze altar for sin and other offerings. Between that altar and the Tent of Meeting, they were to place the second object, the large bronze basin filled with water.

Before the priests could enter the Tent of Meeting, they had to do two things while in the surrounding courtyard. First, they had to offer blood sacrifices upon the bronze altar for the cleansing of their sins. As Charles Spurgeon points out, this is just as necessary for us today—though it is in the precious blood of Christ that we need to wash daily, not in the blood of sheep and goats:

> If you have ever come to the blood of sprinkling, you will feel your need of coming to it

every day. He who does not desire to wash in it
every day has never washed in it at all. The believer always feels it to be his joy and privilege
that there is still a fountain opened.... This
morning let us sprinkle our doorposts fresh
with blood, and then, feast on the lamb, as-
sured that the destroying angel must pass us
by.[7]

Second, the priests had to wash their hands and feet using
the water in the large bronze basin that was placed within
the courtyard between the bronze altar and the Tent of
Meeting:

Then the LORD spoke to Moses, saying: "You
shall also make a laver of bronze, with its base
also of bronze, for washing. You shall put it between the tabernacle of meeting and the altar.
And you shall put water in it, for Aaron and
his sons shall wash their hands and their feet
in water from it. When they go into the tabernacle of meeting, or when they come near the
altar to minister, to burn an offering made by
fire to the LORD, they shall wash with water,
lest they die. So they shall wash their hands
and their feet, lest they die. And it shall be a
statute forever to them—to him and his de-
scendants throughout their generations." (Exodus 30:17–21)

Steve Fenchel then stated that Christians today often
speak of cleansing from sin through the sacrifice of blood,

but forget about the New Testament fulfillment of washing in the bronze basin—before we enter into the presence of the Lord.

As 1 John 5:6 states, "This is He who came by water and blood—Jesus Christ; not only by water, but by water and blood." If the sacrifice of the blood of Jesus washes away our sins, there is a second washing that is also necessary. Ephesians 5:25–26 declares, "…Christ also loved the church and gave Himself for her, that He might sanctify and cleanse her with the washing of water by the word…." This Jewish minister of the Gospel then declared that, whereas the blood of the Messiah washes away our sins, spending time daily in the Word of God cleanses our hearts and minds from the defilement of the world. In the case of the priests of old, those parts that most came into contact with the world—their hands and their feet—had to be washed in water before they could safely enter the Tent of Meeting. Even so we today need to be careful to wash regularly in the water of God's Word, lest we enter presumptuously into His presence. We need the Word of God to fill our hearts and minds, as well as to drive out worldly contamination, if we are to dwell in the presence of our Lord and serve Him effectively.[8]

# 6    *Character and Community*

The foundation for becoming a disciple is having a direct relationship with the Lord. But this does not mean acting like little self-centered tyrants, lording our opinions and privileges over others as some do. As modern Western society has wandered farther and farther away from its Biblical roots, even believers and some ministries now focus chiefly upon "I." If believers in earlier centuries focused mainly upon building Christian *character* and *community*, many in our day seem to focus more upon Christian success: my life, my ministry, my achievements for God. Yet the Bible calls us back to the culture of "we" and "us." The church was never intended to be a "filling station" we visit once or twice a week—then go about our business for the rest of the time.

Some may treat the church of Jesus Christ as an afterthought, but God places it at the very core of His eternal plan, designed before the beginning of time. The church is and will be no less than *the household of the living God*, His dwelling place—now and forever. Do we truly understand how important the church is to God, how carefully He planned its design? If He was careful with the construction of the earthly tabernacle which no longer exists, would He not also be careful about the design and construction of His church, the eternal Body of Christ? Paul declares in Romans 8:18–21 that all creation is waiting to see the revelation of the glorious liberty of the church:

> I consider that our present sufferings are not worth comparing with the glory that will be revealed in us. The creation waits in eager expectation for the sons of God to be revealed. For the creation was subjected to frustration, not by its own choice, but by the will of the one who subjected it, in hope that the creation itself will be liberated from its bondage to decay and brought into *the glorious freedom of the children of God.* (NIV, emphasis added)

Oh, what liberty Jesus purchased for us through His death on the cross! Just as the Lord rescued Israel out of bondage in Egypt with great signs and wonders, bringing them into the Promised Land, so we have been redeemed from our bondage to self and sin. We have been granted a spiritual inheritance that we do not deserve.

Yet many of us never fully enjoy that inheritance. One of the tragic and puzzling qualities of fallen human nature is that, given the choice, most of us prefer servitude to a *visible* human overlord rather than liberty under the rule of the *invisible* God. We shy away from personal responsibility and accountability before the Almighty, because we would rather have someone else handle our spiritual duties. As the Israelites said to Moses in Exodus 20:19: "You speak with us, and we will hear; but let not God speak with us, lest we die."

*How tragically backwards their understanding was!* Was it not God's intent that His Words to Israel would bring them life? Yet they shied away from hearing His voice—and the vast majority of that generation died far away from God in their hearts. These things were written for our instruction, "lest anyone fall according to the same example of disobedience." (Hebrews 4:11) Yet how many of us today still say, "Let the pastor (or the priest) do it, that's his job, not mine!" Are we that different from the rebellious Israelites? When I was a boy, my father once asked an elder in our church to pray during the Sunday morning meeting. But the man responded in complete shock, *"I don't know how to pray!"*

Have believers really understood what the Biblical pattern for the church is, or have many of them left God's plan buried under layers of tradition? Does the Bible really mean it when it declares that every believer is a priest and king before God, that all are called to be disciples? Someone might well protest that if everyone is a king and priest, won't people do whatever they want? Worse yet, how can you say that local assemblies in the New Testament church had only elders and deacons to watch over them, always multiple, and never one person in charge? *There has to be someone in charge, someone who will make the hard choices!* Many believers today defend traditional Christian hierarchical systems by claiming that going back to the ways of the early church would bring chaos. Worse yet, many never study the Bible carefully enough to realize that the idea of a single pastor ruling over the local church is something that never appears in the New Testament! One-man rule was a development of later centuries—as Christianized religion replaced the original pattern for the church.

Hierarchy and command structures were not new in New Testament times; they were the common way the world worked in government and religion. For those who let go of the Biblical pattern, the alternate, hierarchical structure, lay readily at hand.

How little we understand spiritual liberty, or God's plan for His church! Ancient Israel had much freedom under the judges, *if only they had walked faithfully before God!* Yet they traded their freedom away for a visible, Gentile-style king. They preferred flesh and blood to the invisible, Almighty King—the true ruler of Israel. As the Lord said to the prophet Samuel, "They have not rejected you, but they have rejected Me, that I should not reign over them." (1 Samuel 8:7)

Have some of us forgotten that the Lord Himself is in charge of His church? Are we, like Uzzah of old, reaching out with the arm of flesh to steady the ark of God, forgetting that holy things like the ark and the church are to be handled in God's way, according to the His word and design? This story from 2 Samuel 6 is well worth reading. When David and the Israelites were bringing the ark of God back to Jerusalem, they placed it on an oxcart instead of doing what the Bible prescribed—carrying it on poles borne on the shoulders of the Levites. When the oxen stumbled and endangered the ark, Uzzah reached out his hand to steady it in what might easily be interpreted as a well-intentioned gesture. Yet it cost him his life. God struck him because he had touched an object so holy that no man was ever to lay a hand on it, not even the Levites. They were to hold it by poles passed through the loops built into its sides, thereby affording it far greater protection and stability than an oxcart ever could—and sparing them from death.

When David later again ordered that the ark be brought up to Jerusalem, he rebuked the Levites for not doing it right the first time:

> You are the heads of the fathers' houses of the Levites; sanctify yourselves, you and your brethren, that you may bring up the ark of the LORD God of Israel to the place I have prepared for it. For because you did not do it the first time, the LORD our God broke out against us, because we did not consult Him about the proper order. (1 Chronicles 15:12–13)

How many times have Christians suffered loss because they were not careful to examine God's Word first, and then do things in the way that He prescribes? At the risk of repeating myself, if the earthly tabernacle had to be carefully constructed "according to the pattern which was shown you on the mountain" (Exodus 25:40), how much more should the church, the eternal temple, be fashioned according to the Word of God and not according to human devising?

The great drawback with submitting to human religious authorities and hierarchies, in place of direct surrender to God, is that those officials have no power to change fallen human nature. Submission to them instead of to God can only mask the real problems *with an outward appearance of order.* As Jesus said to the Pharisees, the most religious and *apparently faithful* Jews of His day, "you are like whitewashed tombs which indeed appear beautiful outwardly, but inside are full of dead men's bones and all uncleanness." (Matthew 23:27)

Do these words seem offensive, too strong to describe the present condition of many Christians? Listen to what Charles H. Spurgeon proclaimed to believers more than a hundred and twenty years ago in his message, "Spiritual Revival the Want of the Church,"

> Now, I directly charge the great majority of professing Christians—and I take the charge to myself also—with a need of a revival of piety in these days…. In the first place, look at the *conduct and conversation* of too many who profess to be the children of God…. The evil lies with too many of you who unite yourselves with Christian churches…. It has become very common now-a-days to join a church; go where you may find professing Christians who sit down at some Lord's table or another; but are there fewer cheats than there used to be? Are there less frauds committed? Do we find morality more extensive? Do we find vice entirely at an end? No, we do not. The age is as immoral as any that preceded it; there is still as much sin, although it is more cloaked and hidden. The outside of the sepulcher may be whiter; but within, the bones are just as rotten as before. Society is not one whit improved.[1]

Are we also whitewashed tombs? Or will each and every one of us yield our pitiful all to God, crowning Jesus as

Lord in our hearts as well as in His church? Will we let Him wash us inside and out with His precious blood? May the Lord grant us grace to pray, "Lord send a revival, and let it begin with me!"

You see, the Body of Christ already has a Head, just as ancient Israel already had a King. Israel rejected their King in order to set up human rulers, but they did so at unspeakable cost to themselves and to their children. Shall we set up human "princes" in our churches, or will we as the Lord's congregation submit wholly to the Prince of Peace? He is the only One from whom true peace and genuine order come. Jesus is not about to clean the outside of the cup and leave the inside filthy. He seeks nothing less than to put to death rebellious, fallen human nature by the power of His death on the cross, so that we may walk with Him in newness of life—until, as He prayed in John 17:22, "they may be one just as We are one."

And that is exactly where some of us get stuck. We want the new life Jesus offers, but we also want to hold on to some of the old—just the good things, you understand! As a friend pointed out to me years ago during our senior year in college, not every believer *wants* to give their all to God. Not everybody *wants* to be a disciple—even if it is the Scriptural norm. Some of us just want to live a good life, with Jesus playing an important role, but we do not want Him to be the whole deal. *At least my classmate was honest!*

Sometimes believers find traditional church structures more comfortable simply because things seem to go on just the same whether they are right with God or not. It barely matters whether they have given Jesus their all, or only select parts. As long as *someone* is doing what they

should, especially the pastor, it appears that God contin-
ues to work and all seems well with the world. *So why
should they be bothered?* Yet all along the poor pastor is
bothered, caring about more needs and concerns than
God intended any one person should bear. Meanwhile, the
churchgoer fails to respond to God's call on his or her own
life.

Why does this happen? It occurs first of all because we
have forgotten that leadership in the Biblical church is *always multiple.* No one person will ever have all the gifts of
the Spirit, or all the abilities that God will reveal in His
church. Secondly, we forget that every member is called
to take their place in the Body, responsibly caring for others in varying capacities as the Holy Spirit gives each one
ability, so that no individual is overwhelmed. We are *all*
called to build a godly, caring community in which every
member is concerned for every other member. We are *all*
called to build godly character as Paul insists in Philippians
2:12–13,

> Therefore, my beloved, as you have always
> obeyed, not as in my presence only, but now
> much more in my absence, work out your own
> salvation with fear and trembling; for it is God
> who works in you both to will and to do for
> His good pleasure.

Working out one's own salvation is critical to our growing
up spiritually and becoming like Christ. We cannot save
ourselves, only Christ can, but once we receive salvation,
we are responsible before God to bring every aspect of our
lives into conformity with our Lord and His will.

# 7   *Idolatry*

> Hear, O Israel: The Lord our God, the Lord is
> one! You shall love the Lord your God with all
> your heart, with all your soul, and with all your
> strength.

(Deuteronomy 6:4–5)

If we neglect this great salvation that Christ bought
for us, trouble and even judgment lies ahead. Israel lived
a long time in an appearance of peace and religious righteousness, but judgment was coming—it was just around
the corner. As the Lord warned the Jewish people in
Malachi 1:6,

> A son honors his father,
> And a servant his master.
> If then I am the Father,
>    Where is My honor?
> And if I am a Master,
>    Where is My reverence?
> Says the LORD of hosts
>       to you priests who despise My name.
> Yet you say,

"In what way have we despised
  Your name?"

And again, in verse 8 regarding Israel's offerings at the altar of God,

"When you offer the blind as a sacrifice,
  Is it not evil?
And when you offer the lame and sick,
  Is it not evil?
Offer it then to your governor!
  Would he be pleased with you?
  Would he accept you favorably?"
Says the LORD of hosts.

Just what *are* some of us offering to God? Have we become so overly familiar with Him that we forget the fear and reverence due to His Name? The Kingdom of Heaven is not a democracy. God is not a president or a prime minister, but an Absolute Monarch!

As Isaiah prophesies in chapter 42, verse 8, "I am the LORD; that is my name! I will not give my glory to another *or my praise to idols.*" (NIV) We do not like to think of it this way, but when we refuse to let God be our all in all, we are giving to our idols the praise that is due to Him alone. Our particular idols may not appear to us to be as ugly as those ancient Canaanite abominations, but they are idols nonetheless. The real ugliness is not what the idol looks like, *but our refusal to let God be God in our lives.* That is nothing short of rebellion. As the Lord declares in Isaiah 45:23–24,

By myself I have sworn,

my mouth has uttered in all integrity
a word that will not be revoked:
   Before me every knee will bow;
   by me every tongue will swear.
They will say of me,
   "In the LORD alone
   are righteousness and strength." (NIV)

If every knee, believing and unbelieving, of saints as well as sinners, will one day bow before God, *why is it so hard for some of us to bow to Him now?* Why put it off? Have we forgotten the price that Jesus paid to make us eternally His own? Have we forgotten that we have been invited to the greatest wedding in history? "You are not your own. For you were bought at a price; therefore glorify God in your body and in your spirit, which are God's." (1 Corinthians 6:19–20) In Ephesians 5:25–27, Paul declares,

Christ also loved the church and gave Himself for her, that He might sanctify and cleanse her with the washing of water by the word, that He might present her to Himself a glorious church, not having spot or wrinkle or any such thing, but that she should be holy and without blemish.

Is this my spiritual condition today? Am I without "spot or wrinkle or any such thing" in the sight of God, who knows every thought, sees every action, hears every word, and understands every motive? Seeing that He gave all for me, how dare I give anything less than *everything* in return? Even as you read these words, you have an opportunity to yield to God, telling Him that you want Him to be your all in all, your Alpha and Omega. Jesus stands ready even now to wash us "whiter than snow," and to make us "holy and without blemish."

You see, the most fearful judgment is not when God sends down thunder and lightning, or fire from heaven, or even when He causes the stars to rain down upon the earth. The most fearful judgment is when the Spirit of God, offended once too often, quietly slips away from an individual or a congregation—*and nobody knows it*! Nothing seems to have changed, until it is too late. "When the glory of the LORD departed from the threshold of the temple" in Ezekiel 10:18, who realized what was happening? The prophet himself was personally invited to watch and weep as the Spirit of the Lord left His temple. But who else understood the events or implications on that fateful day? The Babylonians could later burn the physical temple to the ground, but only *after* the spiritual part of that temple had already died when the Living God departed from His house.

Was it only for the sake of the Israelites that 2 Chronicles 7:19–22 was written, or were these words penned as a warning for us as well?

> But if you turn away and forsake the decrees and commands I have given you and go off to serve other gods and worship them, then I will uproot Israel from my land, which I have given them, and will reject this temple I have consecrated for my Name. I will make it a byword and an object of ridicule among all peoples.
>
> This temple will become a heap of rubble. All who pass by will be appalled and say, "Why

has the LORD done such a thing to this land
and to this temple?" People will answer, "Because they have forsaken the LORD, the God
of their ancestors, who brought them out of
Egypt, and have embraced other gods, wor-
shiping and serving them—that is why he
brought all this disaster on them." (NIV)

Such terrible judgment was also foreshadowed in the
words of Isaiah 6:8–10,

Then I heard the voice of the Lord saying,
"Whom shall I send? And who will go for us?"
And I said, "Here am I. Send me!"
He said, "Go and tell this people:

" 'Be ever hearing, but never understanding;
be ever seeing, but never perceiving.'
Make the heart of this people calloused;
    make their ears dull
    and close their eyes.
Otherwise they might see with their eyes,
    hear with their ears,
    understand with their hearts,
    and turn and be healed." (NIV)

Are we hearing, but not understanding the Word of the
Lord because we never stop long enough to pray through
until we really *grasp* what God is saying? Do we see, yet
never perceive what God is saying, because we are too
busy with other things? Or can Jesus say to us as He said to
His disciples in Matthew 13:16, "But blessed are your eyes
for they see, and your ears for they hear…"?

In our generation as in every generation, the Spirit of the Lord is sorting between those who have the appearance of belonging to Him, and *those who truly are His*. Every believer in Jesus should read Malachi 3:13–18 from time to time as a reminder that God and His purposes will never be altered. It is we, with our evil and unfaithful hearts, who need to weep before His throne if we would be accepted of Him as part of His holy, eternal church:

> "Your words have been harsh against Me,"
>> Says the LORD,
> "Yet you say,
>> 'What have we spoken against You?'
> You have said,
>> 'It is useless to serve God;
>> What profit is it
>>> that we have kept His ordinance,
>> And that we have walked as mourners
>> Before the LORD of hosts?
>> So now we call the proud blessed,
>> For those who do wickedness are raised up;
>> They even tempt God and go free.'"

> Then those who feared the LORD
>> spoke to one another,
> And the LORD listened and heard them;
> So a book of remembrance
>> was written before Him
> For those who fear the LORD
> And who meditate on His name.

> "They shall be Mine," says the LORD of hosts,

"On the day that I make them My jewels.
And I will spare them
As a man spares his own son who serves him."
Then you shall again discern
   between the righteous and the wicked,
   between one who serves God
   and one who does not serve Him.

# Part II

# The Body of Christ

# 8 Will You Go with Jesus?

The Gospel is a love story, a story that has not changed since the beginning of time. The Heavenly Father is drawing a Bride for His Son out of every nation, tongue, and tribe—from the Jew first and also the Gentile. Everything of this present, fallen world will pass away, but the Lord and His Bride, the Church, will remain forever. There is an account in Genesis 24 that beautifully illustrates this reality. In this story, Abraham is a type of God the Father, commanding his faithful servant Eliezer not to "take a wife for my son from the daughters of the Canaanites," but to "go to my country and to my family, and take a wife for my son Isaac."

This servant, Eliezer, is a gracious type of the Holy Spirit—doing the Father's will, seeking a bride for the Son and not for Himself. Like Eliezer, when the Spirit of God calls to the Bride of the Lamb, He does not force her to come but graciously invites her. As Rebekah was asked, "Will you go with this man?", so the Spirit of God is calling to us today, "Will you go with Jesus? Will you take this Man to be your husband and Lord forever?" Rebekah willingly responded by faith, "I will go," leaving all that was familiar behind to become part of a family she had never met, and live in a country she had never seen. Will we now also respond to the call of God's Spirit, "I will go," leaving behind our old lives and ways in order to become part of that which will never pass away? Unlike Rebekah, however, we were all born Canaanites which is why we must first be born again, and then be transformed into the image of God's only Son—becoming like Him so that we will be ready to be one with Him forever.

Jesus will have His church, "a glorious church, not having spot or wrinkle or any such thing… holy and without blemish." (Ephesians 5:27) As God declares in Malachi 3:6, "For I am the LORD, I do not change…." If we would be disciples of Jesus Christ and members of His church, it is we who must change because God never will. Numbers 23:19 also states,

> God is not a man, that He should lie,
> nor a son of man, that He should repent.
> Has He said, and will He not do?
> Or has He spoken,
>        and will He not make it good?

We live in a generation in which fashions change constantly, with a rapidity that our ancestors could not have imagined. As the Lord spoke to Daniel about our day, "many shall run to and fro, and knowledge shall increase." (Daniel 12:4) Many do run here and there today, but do they know why they are running, or where they are going, or even why they are alive? Knowledge has increased immensely—yet wisdom and understanding are in short supply. If the entire world seems to be racing forward at a rapid pace, let us never forget that the Bible declares that above all else this world is racing towards judgment.

As John wrote in 1 John 2:16–17, "For all that is in the world—the lust of the flesh, the lust of the eyes, and the pride of life—is not of the Father but is of the world. And the world is passing away, and the lust of it; but he who does the will of God abides forever." One day it will be declared, and sooner than we think, "The kingdoms of this world have become the kingdoms of our Lord and of His Christ, and He shall reign forever and ever!" (Revelation 11:15)

When all else has been burned to a crisp, what will remain forever? The Lord and His church will tower far above what the old hymn calls the "wrecks of time." Shall we therefore fear being different from others because we belong to Christ? Shall we fear being out of touch with our generation, or should we instead be afraid of being out of step with our God? As members of a materialistic age, should we not consider the words of Jesus in Matthew 16:26, "For what profit is it to a man if he gains the whole world, and loses his own soul?" No one ever gets the whole world, but many do sell their eternal souls for a little piece of it. Is it worth it? Should I trade an eternity with Jesus for a few moments of pleasure here? Oh yes, there is a cost to giving our all to Jesus, but the cost of not giving our all to Him is infinitely greater!

## 8.1   ONE PEOPLE

As mentioned before, when it comes to the church, God is looking for the number one—the number of unity. He will never be satisfied with less. The Biblical pattern for the church is very much about community, or digging into the Hebrew origins of the word, about the *congregation* of the saints. The various Hebrew words that are translated as *congregation* have fewer ecclesiastical overtones today than the word *church* (which comes by many steps from the Latin ecclesia, the religiously used borrowing of the Greek ἐκκλησία, or ĕkklēsia).[1] They refer quite simply to the gathering, assembly, multitude, and even family of the people of God.[2] As members of one family, one body, we were never called to step on one another's toes while exercising our newfound spiritual liberty, but to daily lay down our lives for the brethren. Oswald Chambers wrote about us in *My Utmost for His Highest*,

> He wants you to recognize the disposition you were showing—*the disposition of your right to yourself.* The moment you are willing that God should alter your disposition, His recreating forces will begin to work. The moment you realize God's purpose, which is to get you rightly related to Himself *and then to your fellow men,* He will tax the last limit of the universe to help you take the right road.[3] (Emphasis added)

We are so used to living in a fallen, self-centered world that we fall into the same old habits, trying to be like everyone else. But God has not called us to be like everyone else, any more than He called Israel to be like other nations. We are called to be nothing less than the very house of God:

> Now, therefore, you are no longer strangers and foreigners, but fellow citizens with the saints and members of the household of God, having been built on the foundation of the

apostles and prophets, Jesus Christ Himself being the chief cornerstone, in whom
the whole building, being fitted together,
grows into a holy temple in the Lord, in
whom you also are being built together for
a dwelling place of God in the Spirit. (Ephesians 2:19–22)

Our position as disciples is clearly set within the context
of becoming *members* of this larger church, the Body of
Christ. As 2 Corinthians 6:16 states,

For you are the temple of the living God.
As God has said:
"I will dwell in them
And walk among them.
I will be their God,
And they shall be My people."

What greater privilege can any of us ask than to be part
of God's eternal house? People fight over the privilege of
seeing the latest celebrity yet, unlike them, the Lord is no
fading star. He is the Alpha and the Omega, the beginning
and the end of all things. He will remain forever in all His
glory—long after Hollywood's Walk of Fame is gone.

What blessed people we are! But do we recognize the
true worth of God's invitation? Have we forgotten the
parable Jesus told in Matthew 22 of the great heavenly
wedding feast? Will we be among those who quickly respond to the Father's invitation, or will He have to go out
into the highways and byways to find others who willingly
accept His kindness? If we desire to be members of His
church, then we must realize that we are members one of

another, charged to obey the same commands that Paul
wrote to the Philippians in chapter 2, verses 3–4:

> Let nothing be done through selfish ambition
> or conceit, but in lowliness of mind *let each*
> *esteem others better than himself.* Let each of
> you look out not only for his own interests,
> but also for the interests of others. (Emphasis
> added)

God has called us to be disciples *together* in Christ, the
word *disciple* appearing many more times in the plural than
in the singular in the New Testament.

In the Body of Christ, not only are we members one of
another, but we are called to *submit* to one another, as well
as to the Lord Himself. In the *New International Version*,
Ephesians 5:21 commands, "Submit to one another out of
reverence for Christ." The *New King James Version* speaks
of, "submitting to one another in the fear of God." Why is
godly submission so critical? Because without it, the Body
of Christ cannot work—any more than our physical bodies can. Imagine if every organ in our bodies did its own
thing, refusing to listen to the brain, or to coordinate with
the other parts of the body. Death would quickly ensue!

## 8.2   THE TYRANNY OF SELF

Modern culture focuses chiefly on *individuality*, which is
why there are so many lonely people in this world. If everyone lives only for him or herself, where is there room
for community or charity towards others? *The tyranny of*
*self is the greatest bondage of all.*[4] This I can testify to personally! I will forever be grateful to Jesus for rescuing me

out of my little self-centered world. There is much left to be done, but I am so glad that He has been delivering me from the narrowness of selfishness and self-seeking, enabling me instead to live in the wideness and liberty of His marvelous love. You see, what God desires in His children is the blossoming of *personality*—the new man in Christ who fits perfectly with the rest of the Body, living stone joined with living stone by the work of the Holy Spirit. When I was a young college student, an elderly missionary strongly admonished my brothers in Christ and me not to live like "ships passing in the night," full of self-centered ambition. She urged us rather to love and care for one another, sharing both our burdens and our joys in daily, godly fellowship. It is advice that I will never forget, counsel that changed my life. As Romans 12:5 declares, "so we, being many, are one body in Christ, and individually members of one another."

Oswald Chambers wrote profound words about the difference between individuality and personality,

> Individuality is all elbows, it separates and isolates. It is the characteristic of the child and rightly so; but if we mistake individuality for the personal life, we remain isolated. The shell of individuality is God's created natural covering for the protection of the personal life; but individuality must go in order that the personal life may come out and be brought into fellowship with God…. God designed human nature for Himself; individuality debases human nature for itself.

> The characteristics of individuality are inde-
> pendence and self-assertiveness. It is the con-
> tinual assertion of individuality that hinders
> our spiritual life more than anything else....
> The thing in you that will not be reconciled to
> your brother is your individuality. God wants
> to bring you into union with Himself, but
> unless you are willing to give up your right
> to yourself He cannot. "Let him deny him-
> self"—deny his independent right to himself,
> then the real life has a chance to grow.[5]

Shall we hold tightly onto "our right to ourselves," and
remain childish all our days? Or will we say with Paul,
"When I was a child, I spoke as a child, I understood as
a child, I thought as a child; but when I became a man, I
put away childish things." (1 Corinthians 13:11) "Childish
things" include my right to my own life.

In our society, and even in our churches, there is a
great deal of childishness, selfishness, immaturity, and in-
considerateness towards others. These attitudes will never
fit in the Kingdom of Heaven, or in the Biblical church.
They are contrary to God's own nature. In Ephesians
3:10–12, Paul plainly described the critical importance of
the church of Jesus Christ in the plan of God. Was it not
and is it not the Father's eternal intent to reveal His own
nature and purpose not only through the Son, *but through
the church itself*? It was the Father's purpose "from the beginning of the ages" that "now the manifold wisdom of
God might be made known by the church to the principalities and powers in the heavenly places, according to

the eternal purpose which He accomplished in Christ Jesus our Lord."

As we walk in the sight of men and angels, both faithful and fallen, are we truly reflecting "the manifold wisdom of God" as members of the Body of Christ? Whose image do we bear as we pass through life—our own with all its faults and failings, or that of Jesus Christ? Either we let go of our right to ourselves, and grow up into the likeness of Jesus our Lord—or we grasp our lives in our own hands, remaining trapped in what Oswald Chambers accurately calls the "shell of individuality." There is only one way to escape the awful bondage of our fallen nature. Religious activity, good deeds, and even good intentions are of no avail. *As Jesus died, so we must die.* The old life has to be "put off" so that the new life can flourish. The hard, unyielding husk of self must be broken and shed. As we deny our "independent right" to ourselves, "then the real life has a chance to grow," the life that our Heavenly Father has been desiring since before the creation of the world.

# 9    *The Blueprint in the Bible*

In his 1890 book, *A Larger Christian Life,* the preacher and evangelist, A.B. Simpson, discussed his vision for the church:

> He is showing us the plan for a Christian church that is much more than an association of congenial friends to listen once a week to an intellectual discourse and musical entertainment and carry on by proxy a mechanism of Christian work; but rather a church that can be at once the mother and home of every form of help and blessing which Jesus came to give to lost and suffering men, the birthplace and the home of souls, the fountain of healing and cleansing, the sheltering home for the orphan and distressed, the school for the culture and training of God's children, the armory where they are equipped for the battle of the Lord and the army which fights those battles in His name. Such a centre of life and power Christ wants in every centre of population in this sad and sinful world.[1]

Can we agree with the words of A.B. Simpson? Can we ask the Lord to give us again the church as she was in the book of Acts, holy, yielded, sanctified, *active*—and empowered from above? This is the church of whom it was said in Acts 17:6, "These who have turned the world upside down have come here too." Does not the world in our generation also need to be "turned upside down"? As Elisha cried out so many years ago when beginning his service to God, "Where is the LORD God of Elijah?" (2 Kings 2:14) Will we not also cry out so that God will have His way in our generation? "'Not by might nor by power, but by My Spirit,' says the LORD of hosts." (Zechariah 4:6)

If we truly want to build the Biblical church of Jesus Christ—in all her beauty and power—then we must daily take up our cross and die to ourselves. We must pray as Jesus did, "not my will, but Yours, be done." (Luke 22:42) Elisha began his ministry with a sacrifice, burning the plow and oxen that his earthly father had entrusted to him, breaking every connection to his comfortable past on the family farm. He did this so that he would be free to serve his Heavenly Father, letting go of an earthly yoke in order to bear a heavenly one. Will we also allow God to break off our earthly yokes so that we are free to build the Kingdom of God in our time? Great works for God always begin with sacrifice, so that our natural life may be transformed into life that is truly spiritual. As Jesus said in John 6:63, "It is the Spirit who gives life; the flesh profits nothing. The words that I speak to you are spirit, and they are life."

If we hold on to our natural life, we will remain children spiritually, thus limiting the power of God to work in us. Only as we die to the all encompassing claims of our natural life do we truly grow up to become the spiritual

men and women of God that Jesus intends us to be. As
Ephesians 4:14–16 states, God's desire for us is

> that we should no longer be children, tossed
> to and fro and carried about with every
> wind of doctrine, by the trickery of men,
> in the cunning craftiness of deceitful plot-
> ting, but, speaking the truth in love, *may
> grow up in all things into Him who is the
> head*—Christ—from whom the whole body,
> joined and knit together by what every joint
> supplies, according to the effective working
> by which every part does its share, causes
> growth of the body for the edifying of itself in
> love. (Emphasis added)

How many winds of doctrine have swept through
churches in our day? Yet the Word of God has not changed
in the least. Will we remain children in our thinking and
theology, carried along by the latest trend, the latest teaching? Or will we die to ourselves in order to grow up into
the likeness of Jesus Christ? Will we allow the Lord to
make us mature men and women of God, knowing God's
Word, clear in our thinking, holy in our personal lives,
and steadfast in our daily walk with Jesus? Such men and
women, faithful disciples, are greatly needed in the church
today!

Note also that the church is described in Ephesians 4
as a *living organism*—every member having a part in the
functioning of the Body. Not every cell in the human body
has the same function, so why should it be any different in
the Body of Christ? As Isaiah 54:2–3 declares,

> Enlarge the place of your tent,
> and *let them* stretch out
>     the curtains of your dwellings;
> do not spare;
> lengthen your cords,
> and strengthen your stakes.
> For you shall expand
>     to the right and to the left,
> and your descendants
>     will inherit the nations,
> and make the desolate cities inhabited.

Stretching out to the right and to the left is the work of *every* member of the Body of Christ, not just a handful of leaders. When we believers truly become a company of yielded, engaged disciples of Jesus Christ, each serving in those capacities that the Lord has ordained for us, then we will turn the world upside down.

In light of this, consider another passage about the church from A.B. Simpson,

> The figure of enlargement is that of a tent; its curtains are to be stretched forth and its cords are to be lengthened. These curtains are surely the promises and provisions of the Gospel, and they will stretch as wide as the needs of human lives and the multitudes that seek their shelter. The cords are cords of prayer, cords of faith, cords of love, cords of holy effort and service. He bids us lengthen the cords of prayer. Let us ask more, but let the strands of faith be as long and strong. Let

> us believe more fully, more firmly, and for a
> wider circle than we have dared before. Let
> the cords of love be lengthened until we shall
> draw men to Christ with the very cords of our
> hearts. Let our efforts for His kingdom reach
> a wider circle. *Let each of us make the world our*
> *parish,* and as the Bride of the Lamb realize
> that all that concerns our Lord's kingdom con-
> cerns our hearts, "For our Maker is our hus-
> band, the LORD of Hosts is His name, the God
> of the whole earth shall He be called."[2] (Em-
> phasis added)

Each of us has a place, a role to play in the work our
Lord desires to do in this generation. Above all else, it is
time to build God's church on her Biblical foundations,
according to the pattern that our Lord ordained for His
church. We get a clear view of this pattern in passages such
as 1 Corinthians 12:27–28 and Ephesians 4:11–13. They
mention a variety of functions that God has given to the
Church, such as that of apostles, prophets, teachers, and
evangelists. It is these roles, and the emerging New Testament pattern of the church, that we will now explore.

# 10 Apostles

As Paul wrote in Ephesians 4:11, "And He Himself gave some to be apostles, some prophets, some evangelists, and some pastors and teachers...." The word "apostle" comes from the Greek word *apostólous* (ἀποστόλους) literally meaning "one who is sent," an ambassador or a messenger.[1] In the first century, it was neither an ecclesiastical nor a religious term, but simply described a person's function on behalf of the one who sent him. It is clear from Scripture that apostles are men specially chosen by God, ambassadors sent out into the world to build the church, often in places where the Gospel has never gone before. The New Testament church had its roots in the work of Jesus and the twelve apostles He chose. As Luke 6:13 states, Jesus "called His disciples to Himself; and from them He chose twelve whom He also named apostles," though one of them later proved unfaithful.

1 Corinthians 12:27–28 states of the ministries in the church, "Now you are the body of Christ, and members individually. And God has appointed these in the church: first apostles, second prophets, third teachers, after that miracles, then gifts of healings, helps, administrations, varieties of tongues." That the apostles come first in the

church is clear from Scripture. Besides being proclaimers
of the Gospel (Mark 6:12, Luke 9:6, Acts 4:33), workers of
miracles (Mark 6:13, Luke 9:6, Acts 2:43, Acts 5:12, Acts
8:18), and builders of the church, apostles also serve an
important role in teaching and instructing others (Mark
6:30, Acts 2:42). They provide leadership for the church
as a whole (Acts 15:2–6, Acts 16:4), watching over the
spiritual welfare of the Body of Christ. As leaders, they are
always mentioned in the plural. One of those leadership
roles is in appointing elders in the local churches (Acts
14:23).

The Bible declares that the church is "built on the
foundation of the apostles and prophets, Jesus Christ
Himself being the chief cornerstone." (Ephesians 2:20)
That is no small responsibility, laying the foundations of
God's church in a way that is fully in accord with His eternal designs, plans that were formed before the foundation
of the world (Ephesians 1:4). As Paul wrote in 1 Corinthians 3:9–13,

> For we are God's fellow workers; you are
> God's field, you are God's building. Accord-
> ing to the grace of God which was given to
> me, as a wise master builder I have laid the
> foundation, and another builds on it. But let
> each one take heed how he builds on it. For
> no other foundation can anyone lay than that
> which is laid, which is Jesus Christ. Now if
> anyone builds on this foundation with gold,
> silver, precious stones, wood, hay, straw, each
> one's work will become clear; for the Day will
> declare it, because it will be revealed by fire;

and the fire will test each one's work, of what
sort it is.

No wonder the New Testament contains a warning about
false apostles who, like false prophets, distort the Word of
God as well as His design for the church—bringing confusion among the Lord's people.

Some claim that there were and only ever will be
twelve apostles, plus Paul of course. Yet the Bible clearly
states that there were other apostles as well, even in New
Testament times. Barnabas is described as an apostle in
Acts 14:14, "But when the apostles Barnabas and Paul
heard this...." Paul wrote in Romans 16:7, "Greet Andron-
icus and Junia, my countrymen and my fellow prisoners,
*who are of note among the apostles,* who also were in Christ
before me." The words "of note" here are a translation of
the Greek word *episeemoi* (ἐπίσημοι), which means "remarkable" or "eminent,"[2] i.e., these two were important
and well-known apostles. James, the Lord's brother, was
also not one of the original twelve, yet he became a leading
apostle in the church. Paul speaks of him and his role in the
church in Jerusalem in Galatians 1:19, "But I saw none of
the other apostles except James, the Lord's brother." Ironically, the very fact that *false* apostles existed in the early
days of the church confirms that there were more true
apostles in the early church than just the original twelve.

Others claim that the day of the apostle is over. But as
long as the church remains in this fallen world, we will continue to need the ministry of God-appointed apostles in
the church. Paul was not one of the original apostles, yet
he became one of the most critical builders of the church
in history. Ironically, many today are unwilling to use the

word *apostle* regarding modern servants of the Lord, yet
the word *missionary* is universally accepted. What is the
difference between the word *apostle* and the word *missionary*? *Apostle* is Greek from the Greek New Testament, and
*missionary* is Latin from the Latin New Testament, but
both mean exactly the same thing—*one who is sent*, a "messenger", an "ambassador," or an "emissary." Why do we accept the use of the Latin word, but not the original Greek
word?

This is not to say that every modern missionary is
therefore a Biblical apostle. Missionaries serve in many capacities—pastoral, medical, evangelistic, and educational
among others. Yet there have been numerous individuals throughout history who were and are *apostles* in the
true sense of the term. One of the finest biographies ever
written about the early nineteenth-century New England
missionary, Adoniram Judson, is entitled, *The Apostle of
Burma. A Memoir of Adoniram Judson, D.D.*[3] He was exactly that, an apostle who opened up a land that had never
received the Gospel. Did Burma (now called Myanmar)
need an apostle? Absolutely, as many Burmese believers
would gratefully confirm today! Judson not only brought
the Gospel to Burma, but gave that land its first alphabet,
its written language, its first dictionary, and its first Bible.

Paul wrote in 2 Corinthians 6:3–10 that one of the
marks of his apostleship was his many sufferings on behalf
of the Lord and His church,

> We give no offense in anything, that our min-
> istry may not be blamed. But in all things we
> commend ourselves as ministers of God: in
> much patience, in tribulations, in needs, in

distresses, in stripes, in imprisonments, in tu-
mults, in labors, in sleeplessness, in fastings;
by purity, by knowledge, by longsuffering, by
kindness, by the Holy Spirit, by sincere love,
by the word of truth, by the power of God, by
the armor of righteousness on the right hand
and on the left, by honor and dishonor, by evil
report and good report; as deceivers, and yet
true; as unknown, and yet well known; as dying, and behold we live; as chastened, and yet
not killed; as sorrowful, yet always rejoicing;
as poor, yet making many rich; as having nothing, and yet possessing all things.

Yet Paul is not the only apostle who faced great trials. It
seems to be one of the common marks of true apostles,
one that separates them from the false. As Paul wrote in
Colossians 1:24–25, "I now rejoice in my sufferings for
you, and fill up in my flesh what is lacking in the afflictions
of Christ, for the sake of His body, which is the church, of
which I became a minister according to the stewardship
from God which was given to me for you ...."

The main focus of a true apostle is not the building
up of his own ministry, reputation, or work, but edifying
the Body of Christ: "...in my sufferings for you...for the
sake of His body...which was given to me for you." Like
Paul, Adoniram Judson endured much suffering, persecution, and even imprisonment in the course of his labors to
establish the church of Jesus in a dark land. In these days
when so many judge a ministry by its apparent success
or lack thereof, we should remember Paul's words from 1
Corinthians 4:9–13,

> For I think that God has displayed us, the
> apostles, last, as men condemned to death; for
> we have been made a spectacle to the world,
> both to angels and to men. We are fools for
> Christ's sake, but you are wise in Christ! We
> are weak, but you are strong! You are dis-
> tinguished, but we are dishonored! To the
> present hour we both hunger and thirst, and
> we are poorly clothed, and beaten, and home-
> less. And we labor, working with our own
> hands. Being reviled, we bless; being perse-
> cuted, we endure; being defamed, we entreat.
> We have been made as the filth of the world,
> the offscouring of all things until now.

God's ways are not our ways—His economy is very different from ours. What may appear to us as the wasting of a
life is, from God's infinite perspective, the sowing of a life
into the soil of a dying world so that many may be saved:
"Most assuredly, I say to you, unless a grain of wheat falls
into the ground and dies, it remains alone; but if it dies,
it produces much grain. He who loves his life will lose it,
and he who hates his life in this world will keep it for eternal life." (John 12:24–25)

The church today needs apostles—men chosen by
God to proclaim truth, to instruct in righteousness as well
as in right doctrine, leaders who will seek the Lord for the
mind of Christ in our generation. They also have giftings
from Christ to heal the sick and restore the wandering, yet
are willing to suffer and even lose their lives for the sake of
Christ's Body. Who else would we *want* to lead the church
today, remembering that according to the Bible apostles,

like all the other ministries, are to be plural and not singular? *How often we believers in Jesus settle for something less than God's best for His church!* May God raise up apostles in our generation, men who are not self-chosen or self-proclaimed, but chosen, called, and purified by Jesus Himself.

# 11   *Prophets*

Pause and wonder!
Blind yourselves and be blind!
They are drunk,
  but not with wine;
They stagger,
  but not with intoxicating drink.
For the LORD
    has poured out on you
The spirit of deep sleep,
*And has closed your eyes,*
    *namely, the prophets....*

(Isaiah 29:9–10)

If the prophets were the eyes of God's people in the Old Testament, how much more do we need "eyes" to see in our confused and troubled age? Again, some believers claim that the day of prophets and prophecy is over, yet who can contest the fact that false prophets are all around us? Shall we leave the field to the false simply because some of God's people do not understand the role of true prophets in this generation? God forbid! We need all the gift ministries *as well as the spiritual gifts* that the Lord has appointed for the church if we are to become all that He intends.

What do we mean here by "gift ministries"? Remember the words of Ephesians 4:11: "And *He Himself gave* some to be apostles, some prophets, some evangelists, and some pastors and teachers...." The words, "He Himself gave," are the key. *None of these ministries are self-appointed.* But when they are real in the church, it is because God has called and gifted individual believers to serve the Body in critical capacities. As pointed out earlier, these are not titles to appear before one's name. They are living, serving functions in the Body of Christ.

Please also note that prophets are usually spoken of in the plural in the New Testament (Acts 11:27, Acts 13:1, Acts 15:32, 1 Corinthians 12:28–9, 1 Corinthians 14:29, Revelation 11:10). As the Scriptures testify in 2 Corinthians 13:1, "By the mouth of two or three witnesses every word shall be established." There is safety in having multiple prophets, but even then believers are not to automatically accept what is prophesied. They are to carefully listen to what is said and then consider it prayerfully before the Lord, comparing it with the revelation of Scripture. Yet prophecy should not be despised either. As 1 Thessalonians 5:19–21 states, "Do not quench the Spirit. *Do not despise prophecies.* Test all things; hold fast what is good." The normal Biblical response to prophecy is clearly described by Paul in 1 Corinthians 14:29, "Let two or three prophets speak, and let the others judge."

This brings up an important matter, one that confuses even believers. Did not the Lord command us in Matthew 7:1–2, "Judge not, that you be not judged"? Then why is Paul telling us to "judge" prophecy? Many have pointed out the seeming contradiction here. The real problem, however, is confusion about the original wording. There are in fact two Greek words translated identically in English as "judge," but they have distinct meanings that English translations may fail to capture. Matthew 7:1–2 uses "judge" to translate the Greek *krínete* (κρίνετε), which means "to distinguish, i.e. decide (mentally or judicially); by implication, to try, condemn, punish."[1] Yet 1 Corinthians 14:29 translates a variant of that word, *diakrino* (διακρίνω), which means "to separate thoroughly, to discriminate."[2] We are clearly not called to judge others—only the Lord has the right to pass judgment on people. Nevertheless, we are called to use all our faculties to distinguish between what is of the Lord and what is not. As Hebrews 5:14 states, "But solid food belongs to those who are of full age, that is, *those who by reason of use have their senses exercised to discern both good and evil.*"

Learning to exercise our spiritual senses, and common sense as well, is part of the process of growing up as disciples of our Lord. There is never a contradiction between walking in the Spirit and using our minds to the fullest as servants of Jesus—*as long as those mental faculties are entirely yielded to the Lord.* The carnal mind will never understand the things of God, but a mind transformed by the renewing work of the Holy Spirit (Romans 12:2) may be of great use. The apostle Paul is one example of a man who fully used his intellectual gifts for the Lord. Nevertheless, we need caution here. As long as we are in this world, we must keep in mind that the Lord's thoughts are infinitely higher than ours, even when we are at our spiritual best. As 2 Corinthians 4:7 reminds us, "But we have this treasure in earthen vessels," so humility is required for us to maintain perspective.

What then is the normal role of prophets in the Body of Christ? As Paul points out in 1 Corinthians 14:31, "For you can all prophesy one by one, that all may learn and all may be encouraged." But that does not mean that all believers are therefore prophets, as 1 Corinthians 12:29 points out. A prophet is a person who is specially gifted in prophesying just as an apostle is a person who is specially gifted by God for the establishing and building up of the Body of Christ upon its Scriptural foundations. When genuine prophets are present in the church, other believers will soon realize this, just as they did in ancient Israel (Ezekiel 2:5 and 33:33). The words of true prophets *will come true*, tested by events and the actual experience of the church (Deuteronomy 18:22). True prophets will also point people entirely to the true God and nowhere else.

One critical Old Testament warning about false prophets is that, even if their words come true, they are still false if they cause God's people to worship false gods,

> If there arises among you a prophet or a dreamer of dreams, and he gives you a sign or a wonder, and the sign or the wonder comes to pass, of which he spoke to you, saying, "Let us go after other gods"—which you have not known—"and let us serve them," you shall not listen to the words of that prophet or that dreamer of dreams, for the LORD your God is testing you to know whether you love the LORD your God with all your heart and with all your soul. You shall walk after the LORD

> your God and fear Him, and keep His com-
> mandments and obey His voice; you shall
> serve Him and hold fast to Him. (Deuteron-
> omy 13:1–4)

This warning is becoming even more applicable as we enter the last days, for as the Bible warns in 2 Thessalonians
2:9–10, "The coming of the lawless one is according to
the working of Satan, *with all power, signs, and lying won-*
*ders*...." Or as Jesus states in Matthew 24:24, "For false
christs and false prophets will rise and show great signs
and wonders to deceive, if possible, even the elect."

A true prophet is an individual who moves regularly in
the gift of prophecy. The core of all true prophecy is revelation, *knowledge that does not have its ultimate source in the*
*human mind but in the Mind of Christ.* A prophetic word
may serve many purposes. One of these is to reveal the se-
crets of the hearts of men, as in 1 Corinthians 14:24–5,

> But if all prophesy, and an unbeliever or an un-
> informed person comes in, he is convinced by
> all, he is convicted by all. And thus the secrets
> of his heart are revealed; and so, falling down
> on his face, he will worship God and report
> that God is truly among you.

The apostle Peter spoke prophetically in a way that revealed hidden evil in the church when he confronted Ananias and Sapphira in Acts 5:3–4,

> Ananias, why has Satan filled your heart to
> lie to the Holy Spirit and keep back part of
> the price of the land for yourself? While it

remained, was it not your own? And after it
was sold, was it not in your own control? Why
have you conceived this thing in your heart?
You have not lied to men but to God.

If Peter had not spoken these words, two believers would
have gotten away with stealing from God and lying to
the Holy Spirit—while undermining the integrity of the
church by their hypocrisy. In this situation, a prophetic
word of knowledge headed the devil off at the pass.

Prophecy may also serve to call believers to repentance, to stir them up to godly activity, or to reveal callings
of God upon particular members of the Body of Christ
(Acts 13:2). Another purpose of prophecy is foretelling
the future so that God's people may be prepared. An example of this is found in Acts 11:27–29,

And in these days prophets came from
Jerusalem to Antioch. Then one of them,
named Agabus, stood up and showed by
the Spirit that there was going to be a great
famine throughout all the world, which also
happened in the days of Claudius Caesar.
Then the disciples, each according to his ability, determined to send relief to the brethren
dwelling in Judea.

Many prophecies in Scripture regarding future events have
yet to be fulfilled. Knowing them gives us understanding
of our times as well as what lies ahead, so that we are not
surprised or overcome by events!

There are many other examples in history of prophetic
words that delivered believers from danger, and even

at times from death. As the Armenian believer, Demos Shakarian, related, a young boy gave a prophetic warning in 1852 "that a time of unspeakable tragedy would come to Armenia and that hundreds of thousands of people would be killed." Armenia was at that time a section of what we now call Turkey, though it was then part of the Ottoman Empire. When in 1905 this same young boy, now grown up, declared that the time for the tragedy was near, many Armenians fled their homes and left their country in order to escape the coming slaughter, a good number moving to the United States.[3] Tragedy soon followed, for in 1915, during the First World War, the "Young Turk" government of the Ottoman Empire carried out a systematic genocide that took the lives of about one and a half million Armenians.[4] Among those who perished were believers who also had heard the prophetic warnings, but who ignored them to their own loss.

# 12    Evangelists

> And He Himself gave some to be apostles, some
> prophets, *some evangelists*...

Ephesians 4:11

---

The word "evangelist" comes from the Greek *euange-listés* (εναγγελιστής), meaning one who announces "good news" or a "good message," i.e., a preacher or proclaimer of the Gospel.[1] It appears only a few times in the New Testament (Acts 21:8, Ephesians 4:11, 2 Timothy 4:5), but evangelists have played a critical role throughout the history of the church. When Philip is first introduced in Acts 6:5 as one of those chosen to be a deacon, or even in the verses about his ministry to the Samaritans and to the Ethiopian eunuch in Acts 8, he is never described as an evangelist. Yet Acts 21:8 plainly tells us that this is exactly what he was: "On the next day we who were Paul's companions departed and came to Caesarea, and entered the house of Philip the evangelist, who was one of the seven, and stayed with him." The phrase "one of the seven" refers to Philip's having been chosen as one of the seven deacons in the church in Jerusalem in Acts 6:5.

The fact that Philip was both a deacon and an evangelist is one of many examples of one individual fulfilling more than one role in the church. As *Matthew Henry's Commentary* points out, this was "not Philip the apostle, but Philip the deacon, who was chosen and ordained to serve tables, but having used the office of a deacon well he purchased to himself *a good degree, and great boldness in the faith* (1 Timothy 3:13)" and "was advanced...to the degree of an evangelist...."[2] His calling first as a deacon and then as an evangelist were both part of God's plan for his life, but faithfulness in the earlier role was critical preparation for his latter and greater place of ministry. The same might be said of Joseph, his faithful service in Potiphar's house foreshadowing his later, greater responsibilities as the prime minister of Egypt. Timothy also had a calling as an evangelist, Paul urging him in 2 Timothy 4:5, "But you be watchful in all things, endure afflictions, *do the work of an evangelist,* fulfill your ministry." Being an evangelist may or may not have been Timothy's primary calling, but it was clearly part of the work he was called to do in the church.

The description of the preaching of the Gospel to Samaria in Acts 8 also points out one difference between the role of an evangelist and an apostle. An apostle may well "do the work of an evangelist," as Paul clearly did in Acts 19:9–10, "reasoning daily in the school of Tyrannus. And this continued for two years, so that all who dwelt in Asia heard the word of the Lord Jesus, both Jews and Greeks." What an evangelistic campaign that was! Yet an evangelist does not fulfill all the roles of an apostle, as we see in Acts 8. When Philip had completed his part of the work in Samaria, leading many to Christ, there was more that remained to be done. Acts 8:14–15 states, "Now when the apostles who were at Jerusalem heard that Samaria had received the word of God, they sent Peter and John to them....." Following up on what Philip had done, the apostles recognized that the new converts needed instruction in the Scriptures. They also needed to be baptized in the Holy Spirit, and required deliverance from the challenge of false spirituality presented by Simon the sorcerer. This work having been completed, the apostles Peter and John left Samaria and went on to preach in other villages that Philip had not reached (Acts 8:25) as they returned to Jerusalem.

In this sense, the role of the evangelist is clearly defined and might even be described as narrowly focused. True evangelism is a ground-breaking ministry, one whose primary goal is the fulfillment of Jesus' words in Mark 16:15–16, "Go into all the world and preach the gospel to every creature...." Keep in mind that the Samaritans to whom Philip preached were not Jews. They were in fact despised by the Jews for having a mixed Jewish and Gentile ancestry, as well as mixed religious practices. Philip's season in Samaria was therefore the first time in the book of Acts that the Good News was preached to a large number of non-Jews, foreshadowing Peter's preaching in Cornelius's house to people who had no claim to Jewishness whatsoever.

The core calling of an evangelist is to clearly proclaim the Gospel in order to bring sinners to repentance and into a new, living relationship with Jesus. Their primary goal is not to instruct believers but to preach to unbelievers—and to do so in a way that draws people to Jesus. Dwight Moody is a perfect example of this highly focused calling. At the Chicago exposition of 1893, there was a "World Par-

liament of Religions" with representatives from many religions, old and new, publically presenting their teachings
for all to hear. If possible, these religious luminaries hoped
to work together to come up with a new, unified religion
for the world. When Dwight Moody's friends begged him
to verbally attack that Parliament, he refused saying, "I am
going to make Jesus Christ so attractive that men will turn
to Him."[3] He stayed out of the fray of contemporary religious debate, and led untold thousands to simple faith in
Christ.

All of the ministries listed in Ephesians 4:11 enrich the
Body of Christ in different but absolutely necessary ways.
Without evangelists, the church may become too narrowly
focused upon the welfare of the redeemed. Imagine, for example, how different the history of the church would be
over the last three centuries if there had been no George
Whitefield or John Wesley, no Charles Finney, no Dwight
Moody, no Billy Sunday or Billy Graham. Whitefield, the
great English evangelist, was once heard to exclaim, "O
Lord, give me souls, or take my soul!"[4] Sadly, not all believers are so moved by the condition of the lost. In fact,
saints too quickly become so comfortable in their personal
enjoyment of God's blessings that they pay little attention
to the dying souls all around them.

This brings us to another critical purpose for God's
placing evangelists in the Body of Christ. He uses them
to stir the church out of comfortable smugness—until believers also take up the burden for the salvation of the lost.
As Psalm 68:11 declares, "The Lord gave the word; great
was the company of those who proclaimed it." But if God
uses evangelists to stir up the church to pray for and then
minister to the lost, He also moves the church to pray for

God's power to be fully expressed in the ministry of evangelists. In fact, the prayers of the saints are necessary to the success of all ministries, but especially to the work of apostles and evangelists. To quote from *Prayer and Evangelism* by Jessie Penn-Lewis, a woman who played an important role in the Welsh Revival together with the evangelist Evan Roberts,

> It is a great help to know that Paul prayed that doors of utterance might be given to him, and that "the Word may run" (2 Thessalonians 3:1). How can the Word "run" when you do not pray for it? It is prayer that sends it "running." Do you pray like this for God's messengers and their message? Pray for all those who are entrusted with God's messages. Pray that they may be "delivered from the disobedient"; that they may be accepted with their message; that they may go only where they are sent by God…. When the pressure comes upon them, and they despair even of life, pray for them—they need someone else to pray them "through." Pray that "doors of utterance may be given" for God's messengers of the cross, and liberty to give the message.[5]

What a powerful and accurate description of the true work of ministry (service) in the Body of Christ! Here is no self-seeking, no personal ambition or agenda, no desire to be number one in the house of the Lord. Here each believer is called to stand for others in prayer until the Lord's purposes are fulfilled. Not all are called to be apostles, prophets, evangelists, pastors, or teachers. Yet every member of Christ's Body is called to uphold the work of the Lord in prayer, to stand prayerfully behind these servants of Christ as they labor for the benefit of the church and the world at large.

And here we come to a truly critical matter in the life of the church, one which receives far too little attention. As Jessie Penn-Lewis also writes,

> Many are willing to give themselves to the work of *talking*—but how few to the work of *praying*? If you will stand at the back of someone you see has a real message and pray, "Lord, give him utterance, let Thy Word run"—that is the WORK of prayer.[6]

Many of us want to *do something*, or to *be somebody*! Oh, how human this attitude is! Yet how few of us are willing to devote ourselves to prayer and intercession for others, standing in a hidden place out of men's sight while crying out to God that His plans be fulfilled on earth. Even more to the point, how few of us are willing to give ourselves to prayer for *someone else's ministry*!

Have we understood yet that it really *isn't* someone else's ministry, that all true service comes from God and not from men? The core purpose of genuine ministry is building up the church of Jesus, not advancing someone's spiritual career. As Romans 11:29 states regarding the Jewish people, "For the gifts and the calling of God are irrevocable," so it is with God's calling of members of His Body to particular places of service. Not all are called to be evangelists, but every member of Christ's Body can pray for those who are so called. The names of Wesley, Whitefield, Finney, Moody, Evan Roberts, Billy Sunday, and Billy Graham are well known among believers today. But how many remember that there were legions of prayer warriors behind every one of these evangelists?

Without these unknown intercessors, the ministry of even famous evangelists would have been far less effective. In 1 Samuel 30:24-25, King David made a decree for Israel that remains true to this day, "But as his part is who goes down to the battle, so shall his part be who stays by the supplies; they shall share alike." No human army can survive without supplies, and neither can apostles, evangelists, missionaries or any other servants of God. God knows this, and no unknown prayer warrior whose intercession becomes part of God's supply line will fail to gain an eternal reward just because nobody in this life has heard of him or her. "But many who are first will be last, and the last first." (Matthew 19:30)

# 13   *Pastors (Shepherds)*

And He Himself gave some to be apostles, some prophets, some evangelists, and some *pastors* and teachers...

(Ephesians 4:11)

No ministry described in Ephesians 4:11 has been more altered or embellished by tradition than that of "pastors." It is therefore critical that we examine exactly what the Bible does and does not say about this place of service in the church. The Greek word here translated into English as pastors (plural) is *poiménas* (ποιμένας), actually meaning "shepherds."[1] The *King James Version* of 1611 translated this word into English as "pastors" for the first time in Ephesians 4:11. This is the only place where the English word "pastors" appears in the Bible. Everywhere else, even in the *King James Version, poimen* is translated as "shepherd," or "shepherds" in the plural. Of the 16 places other than Ephesians 4:11 that this Greek word appears, it is always referring either to actual shepherds who care for real sheep (as in Luke 2:8, 15, 18, 20 or Matthew 26:31), or it is being used to describe Jesus Himself in His function as the shepherd of God's sheep (as in Hebrews 13:20 or 1 Peter 5:4).²

Thus, this ministry listed in Ephesians 4:11 *of which more is made today than all the other four combined* appears in noun form only once in the New Testament. Our chief clue as to what the function of the *poiménas* (shepherds) was in New Testament days comes from two other places. In these, the same word appears not as a noun but as a verb, i.e., a *function*.³ In Acts 20:28, Paul is giving his farewell speech to the Ephesian elders and specifically says to them,

> Therefore take heed to yourselves and to all the flock, among which the Holy Spirit has made you overseers, *to shepherd* the church of God which He purchased with His own blood. (Emphasis added)

The Greek word translated here as "to shepherd" is *poimaínein* (ποιμαίνειν). It means "to tend as a shepherd," though it is translated in the *King James Version* as "to feed."⁴

The second passage that contains this word is 1 Peter 5:2, though we will quote verses 1–4 in order to give the context:

> The elders who are among you I exhort, I who am a fellow elder and a witness of the sufferings of Christ, and also a partaker of the glory that will be revealed: *Shepherd* the flock of God which is among you, serving as overseers, not by compulsion but willingly, not for dishonest gain but eagerly; nor as being lords

over those entrusted to you, but being examples to the flock; and when the Chief Shepherd appears, you will receive the crown of
glory that does not fade away.

The Greek word used here, *poimánate* (ποιμάνατε), is the
plural command form of the same verb used in Acts
20:28.[5]

Interestingly enough, this word does appear in verb
form in two other places, once referring to Peter, and the
other referring to Jesus Himself.[6] The first of these is John
21:16 when Jesus was restoring a repentant Peter to his
place in the Body of Christ. This is a fascinating passage,
so we will quote all of John 21:15–17:

So when they had eaten breakfast, Jesus said
to Simon Peter, "Simon, son of Jonah, do you
love Me more than these?" He said to Him,
"Yes, Lord; You know that I love You." He said
to him, "*Feed* My lambs.

He said to him again a second time, "Simon,
son of Jonah, do you love Me?" He said to
Him, "Yes, Lord; You know that I love You."
He said to him, "*Tend* My sheep."

He said to him the third time, "Simon, son of
Jonah, do you love Me?" Peter was grieved because He said to him the third time, "Do you
love Me?" And he said to Him, "Lord, You
know all things; You know that I love You." Jesus said to him, "*Feed* My sheep." (Emphasis
added)

In verses 15 and 17, Jesus uses the Greek word *boské* (βόσκε) which means "to pasture, to fodder, or to graze," all having to do with feeding the sheep.[7] But in verse 16, Jesus uses the word *poímaine* (ποίμαινε), the singular command form of the verb we saw in Acts 20:28 and 1 Peter 5:2, meaning "tend as a shepherd."[8] The *King James Version* entirely misses this distinction in the verbs being used in this passage.

The second use of this word in verb form refers to Jesus Himself, and comes from Revelation 7:16–17:

> They shall neither hunger anymore nor thirst anymore; the sun shall not strike them, nor any heat; for the Lamb who is in the midst of the throne *will shepherd* them and lead them to living fountains of waters. And God will wipe away every tear from their eyes.

The variant of the verb form here is *poimaneí* (ποιμανεί), the future tense.[9] When Jesus returns to reign forever among His people, He alone will be the Great Shepherd of the sheep. No other shepherds need apply!

So what do we conclude from these passages? The only places where the verb "to shepherd" appears in the New Testament are in reference to elders and to Jesus. The apostles Paul and Peter directly designate elders as those members of the Body of Christ who are called to "shepherd" the local churches. Once again, please note that elders are always referred to in the plural. As for Jesus' words to Peter, as an apostle of the church, Peter was also called by the Lord Himself to "shepherd" the flock of God. Given what Jesus had called Peter to be and do, please note again exactly what this apostle wrote in 1 Peter 5:1, "The elders who are among you I exhort, *I who am a fellow elder* ...." As an apostle *and* an elder, Peter was directing the elders of the local churches *to shepherd* the flock of God—passing on the very charge that Jesus had given him years earlier. We pointed out before that an apostle may also function at times as a prophet or as an evangelist, but now we see an apostle functioning as an elder as well.

So where did the current role of a *pastor* as the chief executive officer of the local church come from? One strong hint is found in the origin of the word "pastor" itself. It is neither a Hebrew nor a Greek word, but comes directly from the Latin word *pāstor* which means... shepherd![10] When the original multiple ministries in the New Testament church began to be replaced by a hierarchy of individuals in leadership positions, what had been a plural group of elders or shepherds (*pastors* in Latin) appointed in each local church was replaced by a single "priest" or "pastor." The word "pastor" became the title of the appointed leader of each local parish in what would develop into the official Roman church.

Additionally, one of the original roles of the New Testament elders, that of overseer, was transliterated into Latin as *episcopus* which later was rounded down to *bishop* in English, and transformed into the title of one individual overseeing a region with all its parish priests (pastors). Place the Greek prefix "arch" (from *archo*, chief ruler or principal) before the word bishop and you have another hierarchical title, *arch-bishop*, one who rules over the bishops. The titles of *cardinal*[11] and *pope* have their origins in the Roman Empire and not in the Bible. In the end, what had been the living *organism* of the Body of Christ with all of its rich and varied functions—and spiritual liberty—was supplanted by the *organization* of a religious institution.

The problem with religious *organizations* is that they tend to take on a life of their own, even when the life of the Spirit is diminished or absent within them. More than that, officials in both secular and religious organizations find themselves pressured to defend and justify their positions—or risk losing their prerogatives and privileges. Unless religious leaders are willing to lose everything so that God may have His way, protecting position and privilege may at times place them in direct conflict with the express purposes of God. This occurred with some of the religious leaders of Jesus' day, and it has happened many times since.

Given the fallen human nature with which all of us are afflicted, self-interest may easily push aside our concern for the Lord's interests. Is it any wonder therefore that Jesus said to His disciples, "If anyone desires to come after Me, let him deny himself, and take up his cross, and follow Me. For whoever desires to save his life will lose it, but whoever loses his life for My sake will find it." (Matthew 16:24–25) Ironically, the *King James Version* of the Bible was in part created as a reaction to William Tyndale's translation of the Bible, the first major English translation directly out of the original Hebrew and Greek. Church hierarchies in England were incensed that Tyndale had used no ecclesiastical language in his translation of the New Testament—thus threatening their titled positions! He simply translated the Greek words describing the various ministries in the early church as the unadorned functions that they in fact were, no titles involved. His translation of Ephesians 4:11 reads,

And the very same made some apostles, some
prophets, some evangelists some shepherds,
some teachers... [12]

As for 1 Peter 5:2, which includes the word "overseer"
(*episkópous*, επισκόπους) from which the hierarchical title of bishop was later derived, Tyndale correctly translates
this simply as an *action* rather than a title,

The elders which are among you, I exhort,
which am also an elder and a witness of the
afflictions of Christ, and also a partaker of the
glory that shall be opened: see that ye feed
Christ's flock which is among you, taking the
oversight of them, not as though ye were compelled thereto, but willingly: not for the desire of filthy lucre, but of a good mind: not
as though ye were lords over the parishes: but
that ye be an example to the flock. [13]

Much more could be said using Tyndale's translation, but
please note here the use of the phrase, "not as though ye
were lords over the parishes: but that ye be an example to
the flock." As Jesus plainly warned His disciples, those who
serve in ministry in the Body of Christ are not to be lords
over, but servants of God's people. How quickly that concept was forgotten or ignored after the first century AD!
Those who had once been servants became "lords" of the
church in every sense of the term, at great cost to the people of God and their liberty in Christ. As mentioned earlier, 1 Corinthians 7:23 commands, "You were bought at a
price; do not become slaves of men."

We will speak more about the elders of the church later—as well as about their call to "shepherd the flock of God which is among you." (1 Peter 5:2)

# 14    Teachers

There has been debate about whether shepherds and teachers, or pastors and teachers if you will, are two separate ministries or one calling containing both roles. Interestingly enough, 1 Corinthians 12:28 states, "And God has appointed these in the church: first apostles, second prophets, third teachers, after that miracles, then gifts of healings, helps, administrations, varieties of tongues." This list does include the role of a teacher, but does not mention that of the shepherd. As in all of God's creations, there is a variety and a fluidity of ministries within the Body of Christ, yet also exactness and great care in God's pattern for His church.

The most commonly used word for teacher in the Greek New Testament is *didaskalŏs* (διδάσκαλος, didas´-ka-los), which means "an instructor—doctor, master, teacher."[1] This word appears both in the singular and plural in the Gospels as well as in the other parts of the New Testament. In 1 Timothy 2:5–7, Paul speaks of himself as a teacher:

> For there is one God and one Mediator between God and men, the Man Christ Jesus,

> who gave Himself a ransom for all, to be tes-
> tified in due time, for which I was appointed
> a preacher and an apostle—I am speaking the
> truth in Christ and not lying—a *teacher* of the
> Gentiles in faith and truth.

Here Paul speaks of himself in the multiple roles of
preacher, apostle, and now also as a teacher, especially
of the Gentiles. He states this again in 2 Timothy 1:11,
"to which I was appointed a preacher, an apostle, and a
*teacher* of the Gentiles." Preacher here is the secular Greek
word, *kērux* (κήρυξ, kay-roox), meaning a "herald,"[2] an "official … who made announcements or carried messages on
behalf of a ruler."[3] Paul uses it as a common metaphor, but
it is not a religious term in the first century.

Clearly from these passages, the work of an apostle
may include serving as a teacher, just as we have already
seen them functioning as prophets, evangelists, or even as
elders of the church. In particular, we see multiple apostles
serving in the role of teachers in Acts 2:41–42, following
the many conversions on the day of Pentecost,

> Then those who gladly received his word
> were baptized; and that day about three thou-
> sand souls were added to them. And they
> continued steadfastly in the apostles' doctrine
> and fellowship, in the breaking of bread, and
> in prayers.

The word translated here as "doctrine" is *didachē* (διδαχή,
referring to the act of "instruction" or "teaching"),[4] from
which is drawn our modern word *didactic*. Like the Greek

word for teacher (did-as-ka-los, διδάσκαλος), it is drawn from the Greek verb meaning "to teach" (didaskō, διδάσκω, meaning "to cause to learn" or "to teach").[5] With so many added to the church in one day, someone had to instruct all those converts in their newfound faith. And that is exactly what the apostles in Jerusalem did.

Yet there are others who are called to be teachers besides apostles. This is what both Ephesians 4:11 and 1 Corinthians 12:28 are chiefly referring to, since teachers are listed as a separate entity from apostles: "And God has appointed these in the church: first apostles, second prophets, third *teachers*...." Regarding one local church or congregation, Acts 13:1–2 states, "Now in the church that was at Antioch there were certain prophets and *teachers*: Barnabas, Simeon who was called Niger, Lucius of Cyrene, Manaen who had been brought up with Herod the tetrarch, and Saul." It may or may not be that all of these men functioned in both roles, yet if they did, prophets serving as teachers of Scriptural truth appear in the Old Testament as well. In any case Saul, one of these "prophets and teachers," would later go on to become one of the greatest apostles in the history of the church.

It is also clear from various references in Scripture that at least some elders in the local churches also played an important role as teachers. All those qualified as elders in the churches needed to be able to teach as is shown in 1 Timothy 3:2–3 (NIV),

> Now the overseer must be above reproach, the husband of but one wife, temperate, self-controlled, respectable, hospitable, *able to teach*, not given to drunkenness, not violent

but gentle, not quarrelsome, not a lover of money.

We have already seen from 1 Peter 5:2 that it is the elders who are responsible for the oversight of the local churches, though we will examine this matter further later. It would make sense that such men would need to be able to teach others as part of their duties, as those responsible for the care of God's flock.

Yet it also appears that some elders were especially gifted by God as teachers. Paul writes in 1 Timothy 5:17, "Let the elders who rule well be counted worthy of double honor, *especially those who labor in the word and doctrine*." The word "doctrine" here is translated from another related Greek word, *didaskalia* (διδασκαλία) or "teaching," referring specifically to the *information being taught* rather than the act of teaching.[6] These elders in the churches were especially called and/or gave themselves to the study of God's Word, in turn carefully teaching others what they had learned. Such men are also spoken of by Paul in 2 Timothy 2:2: "And the things that you have heard from me among many witnesses, commit these to faithful men who will be able to teach others also."

Other members of the Body of Christ may also teach at times, yet not have a specific calling as teachers, just as all may prophesy yet not all are prophets: "Are all apostles? Are all prophets? Are all teachers?" (1 Corinthians 12:29) Regarding the meeting together of members of the local church, Paul wrote in 1 Corinthians 14:26 (NIV), "What then shall we say, brothers? When you come together, everyone has a hymn, or a *word of instruction*, a revelation, a tongue or an interpretation." A "word of instruction" comes from the Greek work *didacheén* (διδαχην, or "doctrine", or a "teaching"),[7] showing that in any given gathering of the church, the Holy Spirit may give different members of the Body something to teach the others for the edification of all.

Paul also specifically describes the role of teaching that older believing women should have in the everyday lives of younger women in the church,

> Likewise, teach the older women to be reverent in the way they live, not to be slanderers or addicted to much wine, but *to teach what is good*. Then they can train the younger women to love their husbands and children, to be self-controlled and pure, to be busy at home, to be kind, and to be subject to their husbands, so that no one will malign the word of God. (Titus 2:3–5, NIV)

Finally, the writer to the Hebrews seems to indicate that every mature believer needs to develop the ability to teach others, and that a failure to do so indicates a lapse in the normal development of a disciple:

> *For though by this time you ought to be teachers*, you need someone to teach you again the first principles of the oracles of God; and you have come to need milk and not solid food. For everyone who partakes only of milk is unskilled in the word of righteousness, for he is a babe. *But solid food belongs to those who are of full age*, that is, those who by reason of

use have their senses exercised to discern both
good and evil. (Hebrews 5:12–14, emphasis
added)

Here, the writer enumerates one of the key requirements
for anyone who wants to teach others in the Body of
Christ. They must continually exercise all of their senses,
spiritual and natural, to divide between what is of God and
what is not, between what is true and what has only the appearance of truth.

Until Jesus returns, the church has been, is, and will be
in the middle of inescapable warfare with spiritual evil and
deception. As Paul clearly states in 2 Corinthians 10:4–6:

For the weapons of our warfare are not carnal but mighty in God for pulling down
strongholds, casting down arguments and every high thing that exalts itself against the
knowledge of God, bringing every thought
into captivity to the obedience of Christ....

The first job of anyone who would teach others is to bring
their own thoughts, dreams, desires, and hopes "into captivity to the obedience of Christ." To do anything less is to
leave the front door wide open to the evil one. Thomas E.
Lowe, a missionary who laid down his life in Colombia in
1941, used to say that he never wanted his life to contradict
what his lips preached to others. His words affirm what Peter wrote to the saints, "Beloved, I beg you as sojourners
and pilgrims, abstain from fleshly lusts which war against
the soul, having your conduct honorable among the Gentiles, that when they speak against you as evildoers, they

may, by your good works which they observe, glorify God in the day of visitation." (1 Peter 2:11–12) Clearly, one of the marks of a true teacher is that his or her life and words are in full agreement before God, or as David wrote in Psalm 86:11,

> Teach me Your way, O LORD;
> I will walk in Your truth;
> *Unite my heart to fear Your name.*

Above all, a true teacher must first learn from God before he can teach others.

Another requirement for a teacher is absolute faithfulness to God and His Word. Teaching is not a ministry to be entered into lightly. James 3:1 cautions us about this, "My brethren, let not many of you become teachers, knowing that we shall receive a stricter judgment." As with all functions in the New Testament church, those whom God has called to teach others will give account before God regarding what they teach—as well as how they live. Paul warned his spiritual son, Timothy, about his teachings and his actions: "Take heed to yourself and to the doctrine. Continue in them, for in doing this you will save both yourself and those who hear you." (1 Timothy 4:16) The *New International Version* translates the first part of this passage as, "Watch your life and doctrine closely."

Consider the alternative! Teachers who were careless in life and doctrine were all too common in the days of the early church—as they also are today. In one such instance, Paul had to write to Timothy,

> As I urged you when I went into Macedonia,
> stay there in Ephesus so that you may com-
> mand certain men not to teach false doctrines
> any longer nor to devote themselves to myths
> and endless genealogies. These promote con-
> troversies rather than God's work—which is
> by faith. The goal of this command is love,
> which comes from a pure heart and a good
> conscience and a sincere faith. Some have
> wandered away from these and turned to
> meaningless talk. They want to be teachers of
> the law, but they do not know what they are
> talking about or what they so confidently af-
> firm. (1 Timothy 1:3–7, NIV)

People love to be known as experts, masters of a subject
even when they have little understanding of what they are
talking about. This is true in churches, in the world, in the
media, and even in universities and schools. It is one of
those tragic qualities of fallen human nature, one that ac-
cords with Jesus' warning in Luke 6:39, "Can the blind lead
the blind? Will they not both fall into the ditch?" Very often the blind do lead the blind—and all of them end up in
ditches! *Lord, open our eyes that we may walk in the paths of
truth and safely lead others there, also.*

We should note what Paul states in 1 Timothy 1:5
about the qualities of a true teacher: "The goal of this command is love, which comes from a pure heart and a good
conscience and a sincere faith." Those who teach others
must love God *and* His people—"speaking the truth in
love," to use the phrase from Ephesians 4:15. The love of

God living in the heart of the teacher is the greatest mo-
tivator of all for godly, accurate instruction. The teacher
must also be pure of heart for as Oswald Chambers has
stated,

> My vision of God depends upon the state
> of my character. *Character determines revela-*
> *tion*.... It must be God first, God second, and
> God third, until the life is faced steadily with
> God and no one else is of any account whatso-
> ever. "In all the world there is none but thee,
> my God, there is none but thee."[8] (Emphasis
> added)

If these words seem extreme to you, remember that the
moment a teacher focuses upon someone other than God,
whether out of the fear of man or a desire to please others,
compromises in life and doctrine will surely follow.

Finally, without a "good conscience" and a "sincere
faith," the enemy will gain access to the soul of the teacher
and ultimately to those who are taught. Sadly, this is something that has happened repeatedly in the history of Christianity. False teachers do not always start out false, but at
some point they get off the right track. By refusing to listen to correction, they gradually become something they
quite likely never intended to be. *Anyone who would teach*
*others must first be teachable.* Consider again the warnings
from 2 Peter 2:1–3, 18–19, words that speak specifically
about false teachers in the last days:

> But there were also false prophets among the
> people, even as there will be false teachers

among you, who will secretly bring in destructive heresies, even denying the Lord who bought them, and bring on themselves swift destruction. And many will follow their destructive ways, because of whom the way of truth will be blasphemed. By covetousness they will exploit you with deceptive words.... For when they speak great swelling words of emptiness, they allure through the lusts of the flesh, through lewdness, the ones who have actually escaped from those who live in error. While they promise them liberty, they themselves are slaves of corruption; for by whom a person is overcome, by him also he is brought into bondage.

Watch out for teachers who promise you exactly what you want! And be sure to thank God for teachers who get you angry and upset—because they speak inconvenient truths! The former lead men and women to their deaths along rose-scented paths, but the latter lead people to life with words of warning and correction. As David declared in Psalm 141:5,

> Let the righteous strike me;
>     it shall be a kindness.
> And let him rebuke me;
>     it shall be as excellent oil;
> let my head not refuse it.

Lord, raise up true teachers who will build up Your church on foundations of truth and faithfulness in our day!

# 15   *Elders*

The true role of elders in the church has been lost almost entirely, buried under centuries of church tradition and hierarchy. Most churches today are led by one pastor who serves alone, striving to fill an impossible and exhausting role of being all things to all the members of his or her congregation. Yet who stops to consider that not once is any letter or book in the New Testament addressed to the "pastor" of a church?

Paul's letter to the Colossians is addressed, "To the saints and faithful brethren in Christ who are in Colosse..." (Colossians 1:2) Romans begins with the greeting, "To all who are in Rome, beloved of God, called to be saints..." (Romans 1:7) Both Paul's first and second letters to the Corinthians are addressed similarly, "To the church of God which is at Corinth, to those who are sanctified in Christ Jesus, called to be saints..." (1 Corinthians 1:2) In other places he writes, "To the churches of Galatia..." (Galatians 1:2), or "To the saints who are in Ephesus, and faithful in Christ..." (Ephesians 1:1), or "To the church of the Thessalonians..." (1 & 2 Thessalonians 1:1). James writes, "To the twelve tribes which are scattered abroad..." (James 1:1). Peter writes, "to the strangers scattered throughout Pontus, Galatia..."

(quoting directly from the Greek *Interlinear*),[1] and Jude writes, "To those who are called, sanctified by God the Father, and preserved in Jesus Christ...." (Jude 1) Even Jesus in Revelation chapters 2 and 3 speaks again and again "To the angel (or messenger) of the church...." Where is a single pastor in charge of a local church mentioned in any of this?

More to the point, Paul's letter to the Philippians is addressed, "To all the saints in Christ Jesus at Philippi, *together with the overseers and deacons.*" (Philippians 1:1, NIV) Or, when the leaders of the church in Jerusalem decided to write a letter of instruction to the church in Antioch regarding some troublemakers, it was addressed from,

> *The apostles, the elders, and the brethren,*
> To the brethren who are of the Gentiles
>     in Antioch, Syria, and Cilicia:
> Greetings. (Acts 15:23)

While the apostles were instrumental in the leadership of the church as a whole, it was the elders (also known as overseers) together with the deacons who were the leaders of the local churches in New Testament times.

Elders (by translation from the Greek), or presbyters (in direct transliteration of the Greek), come from the Greek word *prĕsbutĕrŏs* (πρεσβύτερος),[2] meaning no more and no less than "elder," one who is older. Elders appear in both the New and Old Testaments and are a very familiar presence in the Jewish community from ancient times. They were older, more experienced, and hopefully wiser members of the local community who served as leaders. They were neither kings nor tyrants, unlike the "lords"

over the Gentiles, but were a less formal and less inher-
ently oppressive form of leadership, serving their community as respected advisers and leaders. A Jewish elder may
be contrasted with a Gentile "lord" in the same way that
the judges of Israel may be contrasted with the "kings"
of Gentiles. When we who are Gentile believers read the
New Testament, we need to remind ourselves that we are
reading a Jewish document written by Jews for a church
that originally consisted entirely of Jews. We therefore
need to watch out for the filter of overlaid "Gentile" traditions that supplanted and altered the original form of the
church.

As we see in Philippians 1:1, elders are also referred
to at times as overseers (episkópois, ἐπισκόποις), since the
elders had responsibility for the oversight of the church
(1 Peter 5:1–2)—something we have discussed before.
Just as "elder" is a translation and "presbyter" a transliteration of the original Greek prĕsbutĕrŏs (πρεσβύτερος), so
also "overseer" is a translation and "bishop" a translifor-
ation of the Greek episkópois (ἐπισκόποις). Unfortunately,
the transliterations have taken on a life of their own in
the traditional Christian church, which is why Tyndale
chose as much as possible to *translate* and not *transliter-
ate* when he formed his English New Testament. He was
reacting to long centuries of oppression of the common
people by church hierarchies who used titles, supposedly
based on Scripture, to claim absolute authority over the
church. The *King James Version* of the Bible, unfortunately,
restored many of those transliterations at the insistence
of the leaders of the Church of England. They were also
picked up in the *New King James Version*. The *New International Version*, like Tyndale's translation, avoids at least

some of these transliterations.

At this point, it is worth noting what Matthew Henry wrote in his *Commentary* about Philippians 1:1–2, "To all the saints in Christ Jesus at Philippi, together with the overseers and deacons." This writer notes of Paul that,

> He mentions the church before the ministers, because the ministers are for the church, for their edification and benefit, not the churches for the ministers, for their dignity, dominion, and wealth.[3]

These words need to be kept in mind by those who serve the church in any capacity. Fallen human nature is prone to turn a position of service to others into a position of advantage for oneself. Politicians do this and, sadly, so do some ministers!

Remember God's strong warning to the self-serving shepherds of Israel through the prophet, Ezekiel:

> The word of the LORD came to me: "Son of man, prophesy against the shepherds of Israel; prophesy and say to them: 'This is what the Sovereign LORD says: Woe to the shepherds of Israel who only take care of themselves! Should not shepherds take care of the flock? You eat the curds, clothe yourselves with the wool and slaughter the choice animals, but you do not take care of the flock. You have not strengthened the weak or healed the sick or bound up the injured. You have not brought back the strays or searched for

the lost. You have ruled them harshly and brutally.'" (Ezekiel 34:1–4, NIV)

And again the Lord commands Ezekiel to declare,

> As for you, my flock, this is what the
> Sovereign LORD says: I will judge between
> one sheep and another, and between rams
> and goats. Is it not enough for you to feed on
> the good pasture? Must you also trample the
> rest of your pasture with your feet? Is it not
> enough for you to drink clear water? Must
> you also muddy the rest with your feet? Must
> my flock feed on what you have trampled and
> drink what you have muddied with your feet?
> (Ezekiel 34:17–19, NIV)

No wonder judgment begins with the House of God! Self-seeking and self-serving prevail all too often even among the very people to whom Jesus said, "A new commandment I give to you, that you love one another; as I have loved you, that you also love one another. By this all will know that you are My disciples, if you have love for one another." (John 13:34–35)

In his *Commentary* on 1 Peter 5:1–4, Matthew Henry also makes a unique contribution to the correct understanding of the word *kleros* from the Greek Bible, or *clergy* from the Latin Bible, originally meaning "lot," or "portion," or "inheritance":

> The eminent dignity of the church of God,
> and all the true members of it. These poor,

dispersed, suffering Christians were the flock of God. The rest of the world is a brutal herd. These are an orderly flock, redeemed to God by the great Shepherd, living in holy love and communion one with another, according to the will of God. They are also dignified with the title of *God's heritage or clergy*, his peculiar **lot**, chosen out of the common multitude for his own people, to enjoy his special favour and to do him special service. *The word is never restricted in the New Testament to the ministers of religion.*[4] (Emphasis added)

The use of *clergy* to describe a body of ministers who are separate from and rule over the people of God is a development of later centuries, neither Biblical nor characteristic of the early church. God's House is to be one flock, one people, the peculiar lot or inheritance (*kleros*) of God forever, with no division between those who minister to God's people and the flock as a whole.

Matthew Henry also notes regarding Philippians 1:1–2 that it is clear that there were in fact only two offices in the local church in New Testament times:

> *with the bishops and deacons,* the bishops or elders, in the first place, whose office it was to teach and rule, and the deacons, or overseers of the poor, who took care of the outward business of the house of God: the place, the furniture, the maintenance of the ministers, and provision for the poor. These were all the offices which were then known in the

church, and which were of divine appoint-
ment. The apostle, in the direction of his epistle to a Christian church, acknowledges but
two orders, which he calls bishops and deacons.[5]

Some over the centuries have tried to separate out "bishops" (overseers) from "presbyters" (elders) and make
them different offices, but Henry points out that in the
Bible these are clearly one and the same office:

And whosoever shall consider that the same
characters and titles, the same qualifications,
the same acts of office, and the same hon-
our and respect, are every where ascribed
throughout the New Testament to those who
are called bishops and presbyters (as Dr.
Hammond and other learned men allow), will
find it difficult to make them a different office
or distinct order of ministry in the scripture
times.[6]

We need, if anything, to recapture the original simplicity
of the pattern of the Biblical church—so that we may have
the same power, holiness, and liberty as that early church.

Elders were to be appointed in every local congregation, as Paul wrote to Titus: "For this reason I left you
in Crete, that you should set in order the things that are
lacking, and appoint elders in every city as I commanded
you...." (Titus 1:5) Note here that local churches were
identified with the city in which they were located. There
was one church in Jerusalem with one group of apostles

and elders, though it consisted of thousands of believers.
As Acts 2:41–47 (NIV) states of this church,

> Those who accepted his message were bap-
> tized, and about three thousand were added
> to their number that day. They devoted them-
> selves to the apostles' teaching and to the
> fellowship, to the breaking of bread and to
> prayer. Everyone was filled with awe, and
> many wonders and miraculous signs were
> done by the apostles. All the believers were to-
> gether and had everything in common. Sell-
> ing their possessions and goods, they gave to
> anyone as he had need. Every day they con-
> tinued to meet together in the temple courts.
> They broke bread in their homes and ate to-
> gether with glad and sincere hearts, praising
> God and enjoying the favor of all the peo-
> ple. And the Lord added to their number daily
> those who were being saved.

This passage gives a fascinating glimpse into two types of
gatherings of the church in Jerusalem. The first were meet-
ings in which the entire church was present: "Every day
they continued to meet together in the temple courts...,"
as described in this passage as well as in Acts 5:12 (NIV),
"And all the believers used to meet together in Solomon's
Colonnade." There is also a description of an occasion in
Acts 6:2 (NIV) when "the Twelve gathered all the disciples
together," or as the NKJV translates this "the multitude of
the disciples," to discuss a specific need in the church.

In addition to these large gatherings, the disciples also met frequently in smaller groups, "breaking bread from house to house." The larger gatherings are described as times during which the church would listen "to the apostles' teaching," among other things. It would seem reasonable to conclude that in the smaller gatherings from house to house, there was more room for all to minister, as described by Paul in 1 Corinthians 14:26: "How is it then, brethren? Whenever you come together, each of you has a psalm, has a teaching, has a tongue, has a revelation, has an interpretation." In sum, there was room in the early church for the gift ministries of Ephesians 4:11, but there was also room for all the members of the Body to minister one to another as the Spirit led them.

In New Testament times, just as there was only one church in Jerusalem, so there was only one in Ephesus, one in Antioch, one in Corinth, etc. All the later dividing up of cities and churches along denominational lines, as well as the identification of a church with a *building*, were much later developments. And within the church in every city, there were to be elders watching over and caring for the Lord's congregation. Elders were usually appointed by apostles, but behind that human choosing was the work of the Holy Spirit. This may be seen in Paul's words to the Ephesian elders: "Therefore take heed to yourselves and to all the flock, *among which the Holy Spirit has made you overseers*, to shepherd the church of God which He purchased with His own blood." (Acts 20:28)

Paul lays out the qualifications for an elder in Titus 1:6–9 (NIV):

An elder must be blameless, the husband

of but one wife, a man whose children believe and are not open to the charge of being
wild and disobedient. Since an overseer is entrusted with God's work, he must be blameless—not overbearing, not quick-tempered,
not given to drunkenness, not violent, not
pursuing dishonest gain. Rather he must be
hospitable, one who loves what is good, who
is self-controlled, upright, holy and disci-
plined. He must hold firmly to the trustworthy message as it has been taught, so that he
can encourage others by sound doctrine and
refute those who oppose it.

The elders' chief responsibilities were to watch over and
care for the flock of God (Acts 20:28, 1 Peter 5:1–2), to
direct the affairs of the church (1 Timothy 5:17), to make
decisions on behalf of the church together with the apostles (Acts 15:6), to be an example of godly living (1 Peter
5:2), to pray for the sick among the flock (James 5:14),
to teach right doctrine and refute what is false (Titus 1:9),
and to be faithful in all things to God and to the church.

There is a warning that Matthew Henry gives regarding 1 Peter 5:1-4 and the role of the elders (pastors) which
is worth noting here:

> The pastors of the church ought to consider
> their people as the flock of God, as God's her-
> itage, and treat them accordingly. They are
> not theirs, to be lorded over at pleasure; but
> they are God's people, and should be treated

with love, meekness, and tenderness, for the
sake of him to whom they belong.

The church is not the property of the elders, but of Christ
Himself. As those who must one day give account to God,
elders should consider how they treat those under their
care, neither careless on the one hand, nor overbearing on
the other. Love and humility go a long way towards enabling elders to fulfill their necessary duties on behalf of
the Lord's flock.

Before we cite an example to illustrate Matthew
Henry's point, we should once again note that leadership
in the New Testament church was always plural, elders
included. There were *multiple* leaders in *multiple* congregations—affording safety, balance, and a rich variety of
counsel that no one individual could ever provide. The
one starkly contrasting example to this multiple leadership
at all levels in the church is found in 3 John 9–10:

> I wrote to the church, but Diotrephes, *who*
> *loves to have the preeminence among them,* does
> not receive us. Therefore, if I come, I will
> call to mind his deeds which he does, prat-
> ing against us with malicious words. And not
> content with that, he himself does not receive
> the brethren, and forbids those who wish to,
> putting them out of the church. (Emphasis
> added)

Here the apostle decries the actions of a man who deliberately placed himself in a *singular* position of leadership, de-
faming others, and persistently refusing to receive believers visiting *his* local congregation. John's words speak first

and foremost of Diotrephes' *motive*, loving to be number one in the local congregation. John concludes his passage about Diotrephes with the words, "Beloved, do not imitate what is evil, but what is good. He who does good is of God, but he who does evil has not seen God." (3 John 11)

Sadly, Diotrephes' behavior which at the time was such a stark exception has become more common since then, demonstrating why the Biblical pattern of *plural* church leadership is so critical. None of us is complete in ourselves—we urgently need the support and correction of the other members of the Body of Christ. Anyone serving as an elder must especially be on guard regarding motives, because loving to be number one is so strong in fallen human nature. Jesus declared, "But he who is greatest among you shall be your servant. And whoever exalts himself will be humbled, and he who humbles himself will be exalted." (Matthew 23:11–12)

On the other hand, members of the congregations themselves need to be careful to submit to their elders as those who are responsible for them before God. 1 Thessalonians 5:12–13 states,

> And we urge you, brethren, to recognize those who labor among you, and are *over you in the Lord* and admonish you, and to esteem them very highly in love for their work's sake.

The writer to the Hebrews 13:17 commands the people of God,

> Obey those who rule over you, and be submissive, for they watch out for your souls, as

those who must give account. Let them do so
with joy and not with grief, for that would be
unprofitable for you.

This is a critical point, because how every member of the
Body of Christ treats every other member should bring
joy, not grief—yet how often believers fail on exactly this
point.

We should also note before we close this discussion
that, immediately after speaking to the elders regarding
their responsibilities, Peter himself addresses the younger
members of the church:

Likewise you younger people, submit yourselves to your elders. Yes, all of you be sub-
missive to one another, and be clothed with
humility, for "God resists the proud, but gives
grace to the humble." (1 Peter 5:5)

What a lovely balance Peter strikes here! Though the
younger should submit to the older, the apostle also notes
that every member of the Body of Christ must submit to
the other members in genuine humility. None of us is complete in ourselves. As it is with the human body, every
member needs every other member in order to be complete. Pride in the heart and soul of any member hinders
the proper working of the Body of Christ, while humility
is like oil that lubricates every part—contributing greatly
to the proper functioning of the church.

# 16 Deacons

While the elders were responsible for the spiritual needs of the local church, the deacons (διάκονος or diakŏnŏs, literally one who "runs errands," an attendant, a waiter)[1] were responsible for the natural concerns of the churches. As with other terms we have discussed, "deacon" is not a title. It is a function within the church—as the original meaning of the Greek word indicates. In fact, *deacon* is a transliteration from the Greek. The direct translation is simply *servant*. They were servants of the church, literally those who served in what might be considered menial capacities.

Deacons had their origin in a very specific situation in Acts 6:1–6 which pointed out a real need in the early church:

> Now in those days, when the number of the disciples was multiplying, there arose a complaint against the Hebrews by the Hellenists, because their widows were neglected in the daily distribution. Then the twelve summoned the multitude of the disciples and said, "It is not desirable that we should leave the word of God and serve tables. Therefore, brethren, seek out from among you seven

> men of good reputation, full of the Holy Spirit
> and wisdom, whom we may appoint over this
> business; but we will give ourselves continu-
> ally to prayer and to the ministry of the word."
>
> And the saying pleased the whole multitude.
> And they chose Stephen, a man full of faith
> and the Holy Spirit, and Philip, Prochorus,
> Nicanor, Timon, Parmenas, and Nicolas, a
> proselyte from Antioch, whom they set be-
> fore the apostles; and when they had prayed,
> they laid hands on them.

The apostles had their hands full with the spiritual needs
and concerns of the church, including instructing the people from the "word of God," as this passage indicates. They
did not have time for distributing funds, caring for wid-
ows, and other natural needs—*yet neither did they minimize the importance of these matters.* The counsel of the
twelve was that men be chosen who had a good reputation
among the people, who were filled with the Holy Spirit,
and who were also wise in their actions. Someone might
argue that these requirements were "overkill" for merely
natural responsibilities. Nevertheless, this should be a seri-
ous reminder to us that the church of Jesus Christ needs to
handle even natural matters with spiritual wisdom and understanding. Everyday life is far more spiritual than we often realize. Natural situations, if mishandled, can become
opportunities for the evil one—especially in the Body of
Christ.

1 Timothy 3 lays out the requirements for both elders and deacons, those qualifications being quite similar.
Verses 8–13 state specifically about deacons:

Likewise deacons must be reverent, not double-tongued, not given to much wine, not greedy for money, holding the mystery of the faith with a pure conscience. But let these also first be tested; then let them serve as deacons, being found blameless. Likewise, their wives must be reverent, not slanderers, temperate, faithful in all things. Let deacons be the husbands of one wife, ruling their children and their own houses well. For those who have served well as deacons obtain for themselves a good standing and great boldness in the faith which is in Christ Jesus.

Note that deacons must endure a season of testing before they are allowed to serve. In fact, all disciples are and will be tested by the Spirit of the Lord, something we rarely speak of these days. As was pointed out earlier, in emphasizing being born again as an end in itself rather than just the beginning of true spiritual life, we minimize the necessity of growing up in Christ—of the sanctifying work of the cross, and of the building of godly character. These are all necessary in the life of one who would be a servant of the church, for that is what a deacon is.

In 1 Timothy 3, it is worth noting that Paul states that both an elder and a deacon are required to be "one who rules his own house well, having his children in submission with all reverence (for if a man does not know how to rule his own house, how will he take care of the church of God?)" This is a very reasonable requirement for *everyone* in a position of leadership in the local church, whether in natural or spiritual capacities—as much as one can separate these from one another. How a man handles his own family, how he cares for, loves, and provides for his wife and children is a powerful and revealing measure of where that man is spiritually.

The modern so-called divide between personal and public life is entirely fictitious. What a man (or woman) is in day-to-day life in his own home is highly indicative of how he will behave in public life, whether in the church, in politics, or in any other aspect of life. A man who will lie about one of the greatest pledges we make in life, that of fidelity to one spouse "till death do us part," will lie in lesser matters as well. One might also ask, if a man will not diligently care for his natural children, how much less may we expect him to care for spiritual children? It is not specifically stated in Scripture, but we may safely imply from what Paul wrote that both elders and deacons need to have a loving father's heart toward the people of God, *something that is first learned in one's own home.* Sadly, as Paul pointed out in 1 Corinthians 4:15, "For though you might have ten thousand instructors in Christ, yet you do not have many fathers...."

In our own day, how many men and women who desire to serve Christ are aiming to have successful spiritual careers—rather than to become loving, caring, watchful and prayerful spiritual fathers and mothers to the people of God? How much scandal, heartache, sorrow, unnecessary offense, and even turning aside would be avoided among the people of God if those who desired to serve God truly understood what is required of them by a Holy God? How many in our day, like Nadab and Abihu, are offering "strange fire before the LORD, which he commanded them not," serving God on their own terms and not according to His? Those who do so are living in danger of the terrible consequences described in Leviticus 10:2–3 (emphasis added),

> And there went out fire from the LORD, and devoured them, and they died before the LORD. Then Moses said unto Aaron, "This is it that the LORD spake, saying, '*I will be sanctified in them that come nigh me, and before all the people I will be glorified.*'" And Aaron held his peace.

God is holy and those who serve Him in any capacity must be holy. Our need to walk in the "fear of God" has not been rescinded in recent years. As Romans 14:10-12 (NIV) declares,

> For we will all stand
> > before God's judgment seat.
> It is written:
> " 'As surely as I live,' says the Lord,
> 'every knee will bow before me;
> every tongue will confess to God.'"
> So then, each of us will give
> > an account of himself to God.

The church is not our property, but the eternal heritage of our Lord. If a business owner may expect integrity from employees who handle temporal matters, how much more will our Lord require integrity and faithfulness from all who serve Him in eternal concerns?

The consequences of faithfulness versus unfaithfulness in the service of the Living God are nothing less than awesome. How lightly we treat the things of Almighty God despite Paul's warning in Hebrews 10:31, "It is a fearful thing to fall into the hands of the living God." In a day when so many speak of "once saved, always saved," we need to again read the entire passage that closes with these terrible words,

> For if we sin willfully after we have received the knowledge of the truth, there no longer remains a sacrifice for sins, but a certain fearful expectation of judgment, and fiery indignation which will devour the adversaries. Anyone who has rejected Moses' law dies without mercy on the testimony of two or three witnesses. Of how much worse punishment, do you suppose, will he be thought worthy who has trampled the Son of God underfoot, counted the blood of the covenant by which he was sanctified a common thing, and insulted the Spirit of grace? For we know Him who said, "Vengeance is Mine, I will repay," says the Lord. And again, "The Lord will judge His people." It is a fearful thing to fall into the hands of the living God. (Hebrews 10:26–31)

Even in New Testament times, there were already false apostles, and the Scriptures contain many warnings about false prophets as well as false brethren. Many of these began in the truth but turned aside for one reason or another, taking others along with them in their spiritual error. Others were false from the start as Jude 4 states: "For certain men have crept in unnoticed, who long ago were marked out for this condemnation, ungodly men, who turn the grace of our God into lewdness and deny the only Lord God and our Lord Jesus Christ."

No wonder every local church needs multiple elders and multiple deacons to watch over their spiritual and natural concerns! As Proverbs 11:14 declares, "Where there is no counsel, the people fall; but in the multitude of counselors there is safety." None of us are complete in ourselves as the Scriptures make abundantly clear. How many ministers serving in a singular capacity fall unnecessarily into sin because they are not accountable to anyone in their daily labors? They receive none of the reproof, balance, and correction that all of us—young and old—require to remain faithful in this evil, fallen world. And how many are led astray when these ministers fall away?

How awesome are the consequences of the choices we make as servants of Jesus Christ, both for good and for evil! Listen to God's powerful pleadings with Israel in Isaiah 48:17–19, words that apply just as much to us today:

> Thus says the LORD, your Redeemer,
> The Holy One of Israel:
> "I am the LORD your God,
>   who teaches you to profit,
>   who leads you by the way you should go.
>
> Oh, that you had heeded
>   My commandments!
> Then your peace would have been like a river,
> and your righteousness
>   like the waves of the sea.

> Your descendants also
>       would have been like the sand,
>    and the offspring of your body
>       like the grains of sand;
>    His name would not have been cut off
>    nor destroyed from before Me."

The Heavenly Father wanted eternal fruit from Israel, "offspring" whose "name would not have been cut off nor destroyed from before Me." And that is exactly what the Father seeks today! Let us look again at John 15:8, "By this My Father is glorified, that you bear much fruit; so you will be My disciples." The fruit of God's faithful ones is fruit that will remain forever, spiritual sons and daughters who will be "a dwelling place of God in the Spirit." (Ephesians 2:22)

But the fruit of unfaithfulness can and will have no other destiny but destruction, either in Old or New Testament times. No wonder the Scriptures command in Proverbs 3:3–4 (NIV),

> Let love and faithfulness never leave you;
>    bind them around your neck,
>    write them on the tablet of your heart.
> Then you will win favor and a good name
>    in the sight of God and man.

Oh, that the Lord would raise up faithful elders and deacons to watch over and care for the concerns of the Body of Christ in our day, not self-seeking but God-seeking servants of Jesus!

# 17 Other Gifts

Now you are the body of Christ, and members individually. And God has appointed these in the church: first apostles, second prophets, third teachers, after that miracles, then gifts of healings, helps, administrations, varieties of tongues. Are all apostles? Are all prophets? Are all teachers? Are all workers of miracles? Do all have gifts of healings? Do all speak with tongues? Do all interpret? But earnestly desire the best gifts.

(1 Corinthians 12:27–31)

As this passage makes clear, we are all called to be members of Christ's Body, and all of us have a part—as God appoints that part. We as "members individually" need to seek God for all that He has prepared for us, and then take hold of it by faith. As Ephesians 2:10 declares, "For we are His workmanship, created in Christ Jesus for good works, *which God prepared beforehand that we should walk in them.*" These are not self-chosen works, but God-ordained giftings that will bear fruit as we yield our lives to God and dedicate ourselves to His service.

## 17.1  HEALINGS AND MIRACLES

Besides the three well known ministries listed in 1 Corinthians 12:28, Paul mentions other giftings in the church. There are those whom the Holy Spirit particularly enables to be "workers of miracles," performing acts which cannot be done through any natural human capacity. Such works accomplish God's purposes and bring glory to Him in the church—as well as in the eyes of an unbelieving world. Stephen, one of the original seven deacons, is spoken of in Acts 6:8 as a man "full of faith and power," who "did great wonders and signs among the people." Miracles inevitably bring some unbelievers to faith in Christ, because their unbelief is confronted by the power of God. Nevertheless, such works may also result in persecution, as they did in Stephen's case, because there are always those who do not *want* to believe—no matter what God does.

This passage also speaks of disciples who move in "gifts of healing," a specific kind of miracle that brings supernatural restoration of health to those who are sick. These are also spoken of in the list of the gifts of the Spirit in 1 Corinthians 12:9. In Acts 4:29–30, in response to persecution, the church specifically prayed that the preaching of God's Word would be accompanied by healing, signs, and wonders:

> Now, Lord, look on their threats, and grant to Your servants that with all boldness they may speak Your word, by stretching out Your hand to heal, and that signs and wonders may be done through the name of Your holy Servant Jesus.

Some Christians claim that healings and other miracles are not for our day, yet all of God's Word remains true and unchanged. God still heals wherever He finds faith in the hearts of men and women who take Him at His word. Healings not only bring great blessing into the lives of those touched by the Lord, but they cause saints and sinners to stand in awe of God. They also cause sinners to turn to the Lord and become believers in Jesus, bringing enlargement to the church.

## 17.2  HELPS

"Helps" (relief, assistance, support, defense) are also included in this list, something that may seem peculiar in a list of largely supernatural giftings. Yet a little help from believers filled with the love of Jesus has changed countless lives over the centuries, restoring the faith of fainting believers and bringing lost souls to repentance and salvation. A timely help may be far more supernatural than we realize. The Holy Spirit sees a need otherwise entirely hidden from us, and then moves us to touch a soul with aid inspired from above. Even simple helps, when inspired by the Lord, can make an enormous difference. Who of us as believers in Jesus have not benefited countless times from the overflowing generosity of saints moved by God to meet a particular need in our lives: financial, spiritual, emotional, or of another type? And how many unbelievers who appear unmoved by even anointed Gospel messages have had their lives transformed because some servant of Christ showed them a timely, needed kindness? The simplest, least experienced believer may be used by God to

help someone—if he or she has a heart that is willing to
be moved by God's love.


## 17.3  ADMINISTRATION

Another gifting mentioned in 1 Corinthians 12 that may
also appear to be purely natural is that of "administrations" (from the Greek κυβέρνησις, "kubĕrnēsis" meaning
to steer or to pilot).[1] Yet men and women who are skilled
administrators are critical in government, business, education, as well as in the church of Jesus. Daniel and the
three Hebrew children are by no means the only examples
in Scripture of men who were gifted from above in handling earthly matters. Joseph is another powerful example
of a man who made an incalculable difference in the history of the Jewish people by his faithful administration of
worldly concerns.

Jesus' parable of the talents in Matthew 25:14–19 is by
no means speaking only of faithfulness in handling spiritual matters:

> For the kingdom of heaven is like a man trav-
> eling to a far country, who called his own ser-
> vants and delivered his goods to them. And to
> one he gave five talents, to another two, and
> to another one, to each according to his own
> ability; and immediately he went on a jour-
> ney. Then he who had received the five tal-
> ents went and traded with them, and made an-
> other five talents. And likewise he who had re-
> ceived two gained two more also. But he who
> had received one went and dug in the ground,

and hid his lord's money. After a long time
the lord of those servants came and settled accounts with them.

The talents spoken of here are substantial sums of money.
The Bible is very clear that we are called to be faithful
in handling worldly riches. As Jesus states in Luke 16:11,
"So if you have not been trustworthy in handling worldly
wealth, who will trust you with true riches?" (NIV) Only
the Lord knows the full measure of how much damage is
done by Christians who are unfaithful in managing money.

The church today needs people who are gifted and
faithful in administration, again not speaking of a purely
natural gifting, but of abilities which are given to particular members of Christ's Body as the Holy Spirit sees fit.
An able and godly administrator can do much to aid the
work of the Kingdom of Heaven, easing the load for those
who have other callings and responsibilities. Many gifted
ministers of the Gospel are simply not good administrators. It is a mistake to expect them to be something God
never intended. As Romans 12:4–5 declares, "For as we
have many members in one body, but all the members do
not have the same function, so we, being many, are one
body in Christ, and individually members of one another."
We need one another, for no one man or woman will ever
have more than a small part of the giftings the Holy Spirit
stands ready to give to the church. Able administrators of
the King's business are just as necessary to the proper functioning of God's church in this world as are evangelists or
prophets or elders.

## 17.4  VARIETIES OF TONGUES

The last gifting spoken of here is "varieties of tongues," men or women whom God supernaturally enables to speak in multiple languages, both of men and of angels. Or this may be speaking of a variety of uses for the gift of tongues, such as for prophecy, for worship, or for re-buking evil spirits. As the phrase "Do all interpret?" indi-cates in the last part of this passage, the ability to interpret tongues is also a closely connected gifting from the Spirit of God. Some believers are puzzled as to the purpose of speaking in tongues, but let us look at what is clear from Scripture. That believers would "speak with new tongues" was foretold by Jesus (Mark 16:17). Tongues are a sign to a lost world regarding the power and work of God (Acts 2, 1 Corinthians 14:21–22). They are often associ-ated with prophecy (Acts 19:6), but speaking in tongues is only equivalent to prophecy when there is interpretation (1 Corinthians 14:5). Speaking in tongues is also a fulfill-ment of Old Testament prophecy regarding how the Lord would speak to the world as well as to the Jewish people in the last days (Joel 2:28–29, Isaiah 28:11, 1 Corinthians 14:21–22).

Tongues by themselves may also be a powerful form of private prayer and worship for the individual believer, especially when he or she is praying regarding matters which are at best partially understood. As Paul writes in 1 Corinthians 14:14, "For if I pray in a tongue, my spirit prays, but my understanding is unfruitful...." We may not understand what is happening in a particular situation, but the Spirit of the Lord knows. We must be careful to note here, however, that many believers speak in tongues, but not all have the specific gifting of speaking in "varieties of tongues."

## 17.5   WORD OF WISDOM AND WORD OF KNOWLEDGE

There are other spiritual gifts in the church which are spoken of in 1 Corinthians 12:8–10. Besides those already mentioned, there is the "word of wisdom," supernatural understanding given to a member of the church regarding what should be done in a specific situation. There is also the "word of knowledge," supernatural knowledge revealed through the work of the Holy Spirit and not by human discernment. Peter clearly moved in both of these gifts in Acts 5, the story of Ananias and Sapphira. His ability to discern their lying was a manifestation of God's judgment and a severe warning to any believer who might think of acting on impure motives. If Peter had not forcefully withstood this couple, the purity of the church would have been compromised that day. Clearly, believers face many situations in this fallen world where they need supernatural insight into events if they are to carry out God's plans, or to successfully resist the wiles of the evil one. Consider again Paul's declaration in 2 Corinthians 10:4–5, "For the weapons of our warfare are not carnal but mighty in God for pulling down strongholds, casting down arguments and every high thing that exalts itself against the knowledge of God, bringing every thought into captivity to the obedience of Christ...."

## 17.6   FAITH

There is also the gift of faith—capacity to believe for a special work of God in a situation in which such faith is

beyond the scope of others. Remember Jesus' words in
Matthew 17:20, "if you have faith as a mustard seed, you
will say to this mountain, 'Move from here to there,' and it
will move; and nothing will be impossible for you." There
are many moments in the history of faith in which most
believers are stymied by unbelief. But then God raises up
one person, or a group of people, with a faith that brings
about the impossible. To quote from the famous missionary to China, Hudson Taylor,

> Many Christians estimate difficulty in the
> light of their own resources, and thus they at-
> tempt very little and they always fail. All giants
> have been weak men who did great things for
> God because they reckoned on His power and
> presence to be with them.[2]

Real faith reckons on the ability of God, especially when
confronted by circumstances that make our inability
supremely clear.


17.7   PROPHECY

Prophecy is also listed here among the gifts—supernaturally given revelation regarding present circumstances
or future events, or even regarding hidden needs in the
church. We have already written at length about this gift in
the section on the ministry of prophets, and will only point
out here that the ability to prophesy is intended for more
than just those who are called to be prophets. Paul writes in
1 Corinthians 14:1 (NIV), "Follow the way of love, and ea-
gerly desire spiritual gifts, especially the gift of prophecy."

He also wrote in verse 31, "For you can all prophesy one by one, that all may learn and all may be encouraged."

## 17.8  DISCERNING OF SPIRITS

Finally, there is the "discerning of spirits"—the Holy Spirit enabling a believer to perceive and even name the workings of evil spirits in a life or situation where such knowledge is not naturally accessible. A dear friend described this gift as one that includes "suffering," since an individual so gifted must live with the awareness of that evil presence—at least until the situation is resolved. Meanwhile, others without this gift may be oblivious to the fact that something is wrong. Or they may be aware that there is a problem, but not know exactly what it is or what is its source.

Years ago, this author was leading a Bible study in a university chapel when a young man entered. I was instantly aware that, not only the young man, but a demonic spirit had come in. Without fully understanding what was happening, I began to pray in the Spirit against that evil presence, which no one else seemed to sense. Later in the meeting when the young man stood up to speak, I was placed in the awkward position of having to act. I knew nothing of what he was about to say, but strongly sensing the demonic force in his demeanor, I stood up and told him not to speak. At least one believer present that day was offended by my action, refusing to accept any explanation on my part. Yet we soon learned that the young man had actually written out a tirade against all of us that, thank

God, he was never able to deliver! It was not long thereafter that he entered a mental institution, deeply troubled by the evil one.

# 18   Thy Will be Done

As we have discussed, every believer in Jesus is called to become a disciple, something that is abundantly clear in Scripture. As disciples, we are here on Earth to learn from the Lord, to learn from one another, and to learn from experience. If our hearts are set to follow Jesus and do His will, we need to realize that *our circumstances are never accidental.* God has a purpose in every situation, something to teach us or to do through us, something of eternal significance. Christians frequently quote Romans 8:28, but often leave out the final, all-important clause: "And we know that all things work together for good to those who love God, *to those who are the called according to His purpose.*" All things work together for good *when we allow the Lord to work out His purposes in us,* leaving our own needs in His capable hands.

Like Shasta, the central character of C. S. Lewis's *The Horse and His Boy,* the third book chronologically in *The Chronicles of Narnia* series, we are prone to complain when life is difficult. Not understanding why our trials are so arduous, we cry out like Shasta, "Oh I am the unluckiest person in the whole world!" But Jesus replies to us with the words of Aslan, the lion who personifies Christ in

Lewis's tales, "I do not call you unfortunate."[1] Aslan then explains to Shasta how He has been there with him from birth through every trial of his life, turning the most difficult circumstances around for good in ways that can only be seen in retrospect. What Aslan did was not only for Shasta's benefit, but for the deliverance of his homeland, Archenland, as well as Narnia from impending but unforeseen tragedy. If we place our lives in God's hands, He will always make us a blessing to many.

Sad indeed is the fate of those who walk in self-chosen paths, following after pleasing prospects, but never seeking God's guidance. Such souls eventually discover that self-chosen ways always turn into sorrow and ashes. Isaiah 50:11 speaks of what happens when we go our own way, refusing the light so freely offered from Heaven above:

> Look, all you who kindle a fire,
> who encircle yourselves with sparks:
> walk in the light of your fire
>      and in the sparks you have kindled—
> This you shall have from My hand:
> you shall lie down in torment.

These words may seem harsh, but the Bible plainly declares that the core of sin is our assertion of what Oswald Chambers called "our right to ourselves"—that rebellious insistence on being masters of our own lives. The powerful messianic prophecy of Isaiah 53 also speaks of this attitude in verse 6 when it declares:

> All we like sheep have gone astray;
> *We have turned, every one, to his own way;*
> And the LORD has laid on Him

the iniquity of us all. (Emphasis added)

No wonder the Bible declares, "'There is no peace,' says the LORD, 'for the wicked.'" (Isaiah 48:22) True peace comes from God alone! But if we refuse to let God be Lord of our lives, we will miss out on the everlasting, all-pervading peace that the Heavenly Father so freely offers.

The Heavenly Father demands that every disciple of His Son *not* walk in the evil ways of this present, fallen world. How many Christians let the standards of society around them influence, if not determine, how they live and act? As Paul wrote in 2 Corinthians 10:2–6 (NIV), "I beg you that when I come I may not have to be as bold as I expect to be toward some people who think that we live by the standards of this world." God will soon reveal to all mankind, saints and sinners alike, how great and eternal a divide there is between His ways and the world's ways. We are therefore not to fear men or demons, but to fear the One before whom every knee will one day bow.

Near the beginning of this book, we spoke about Isaiah 8:16, the verse in which the word "disciple" first appears in Scripture. Now, we need to also look at the larger passage surrounding this verse. The prophet minces no words regarding whom we should fear—and whom we should obey as servants of the Living God:

> The LORD spoke to me
>     with his strong hand upon me,
> warning me not to follow
>     the way of this people.
> He said:
> "Do not call conspiracy

everything that these people call conspiracy;
do not fear what they fear,
and do not dread it.
The LORD Almighty is the one
    you are to regard as holy,
he is the one you are to fear,
he is the one you are to dread,
    and he will be a sanctuary;
but for both houses of Israel he will be
    a stone that causes men to stumble
    and a rock that makes them fall.
And for the people of Jerusalem he will be
    a trap and a snare.
Many of them will stumble;
they will fall and be broken,
they will be snared and captured."

Bind up the testimony
    and seal up the law
    among my disciples.
I will wait for the LORD,
    who is hiding his face
    from the house of Jacob.
I will put my trust in him.
(Isaiah 8:11-17, NIV, emphasis added)

As disciples of Jesus, we must deliberately push beyond the narrow perspectives of our generation, and take hold of the eternal, unchanging viewpoint of our Lord. How often we are caught up with outlooks that are too small, too bound to earth, so human that they limit the Holy One of Israel? Consider for a moment how Jesus rebuked Peter in Matthew 16:23, after Peter reproached his Master for saying He had to die: "Get behind Me, Satan! You are an offense to Me, for you are not mindful of the things of God, but the things of men." Let us be honest with ourselves as we live our daily lives: Are we minding the things of God—or the things of men?

As we read earlier in Chapter 7, Malachi 3 makes plain that our God will draw eternal lines of demarcation between those who serve Him, and those who serve themselves:

> Then you shall again discern
> between the righteous and the wicked,
> between one who serves God
> and one who does not serve Him.

However confused matters may look from our earthly viewpoint, all is absolutely clear from Heaven's perspective. Blessed is the man or woman who refuses worldly confusion and chooses instead to walk in the clear, eternal light of God's Word and ways.

Let us remember that we are promised peace and every other blessing *only* as we let God have His way in us. We need to keep this truth continually fresh in our hearts and minds. Jesus is not a vending machine, satisfying every need and desire on our timetable. Jesus is the Lord of Lords! He will never willingly take second place in our hearts or lives. As a long-term missionary to Colombia, Mrs. Hannah Lowe used to say, "We are today the sum of what we have allowed God to do in our lives." It is not a matter of what we have done, *but what we have permitted the Lord to do in us.* Blessed is the child of God who surrenders his "right to himself," crowning Jesus as Lord in every facet of life. Blessed also are those who do God's will through each trial and tribulation, not running after worldly rewards but after the Lord Himself. These are the true disciples of the Lamb, *lovers of Jesus and not worldly pleasure.*

All such yielded souls discover in the course of life that Jesus never fails, that every difficulty is turned to eternal good. As the old hymn declares, "It will be worth it all when we see Jesus." Or, as Isaiah writes in chapter 3, verses 10–11 (NIV),

> Tell the righteous it will be well with them,
> for they will enjoy the fruit of their deeds.
> Woe to the wicked! Disaster is upon them!
> They will be paid back
>     for what their hands have done.

What a remarkable promise from our eternal Father! As a young believer, this passage helped me immensely as I struggled with trials and temptations in my life. The end of every *faithful* believer in Jesus will be a good one, which is why faithfulness is stressed so strongly in Scripture. This fallen world can offer no such benefits, failing to deliver even on short-term promises. As for eternity, that is God's domain and His alone. *His promises alone will stand forever.* As for the devil and all his offerings, Jesus laid bare the heart of the matter in John 10:10: "The thief does not come except to steal, and to kill, and to destroy. I have come that they may have life, and that they may have it more abundantly."

Scripture teaches us not to be conformed to the pattern of this world, yet the Lord calls us to remain in the world to be witnesses to Him. As Jesus' disciples, where we go, what we do, and what we say either draws others closer to God or, sadly, pushes them away. Our lives are an open book, read by all, and perhaps the only taste many will have of the Gospel of Jesus. Like it or not, as disciples of Jesus, we are "signs and symbols" to a dying world. May God give us grace to be faithful, bringing honor and not shame to the One whose name we bear! If we are careful to take up our cross, die to ourselves daily, and do the will of God, the Lord Himself will make our lives an eternal blessing to many. As Paul wrote in 2 Corinthians 2:14–17,

> Now thanks be to God who always leads us in triumph in Christ, and through us diffuses the fragrance of His knowledge in every place. For we are to God the fragrance of Christ among those who are being saved and among those who are perishing. To the one we are the aroma of death leading to death, and to the other the aroma of life leading to life. And who is sufficient for these things? For we are not, as so many, peddling the word of God; but as of sincerity, but as from God, we speak in the sight of God in Christ.

What a marvelous privilege God has given us, diffusing the fragrance of His Son to a perishing world through the lives of His children!

Let us never forget what Paul also writes here, "And who is sufficient for these things?" None of us is—or ever will be—sufficient in his own strength. Yet as the apostle wrote in 2 Corinthians 3:5–6, "Not that we are sufficient of ourselves to think of anything as being from ourselves, but our sufficiency is from God, who also made us sufficient as ministers of the new covenant....." In the Biblical sense of ministers, all disciples of Jesus Christ are called to minister—that is to serve. The callings, giftings, or capacities may differ, but service to our God must be the central focus of our lives. And as we labor for Him, may our prayer be the same as that which Moses prayed in Psalm 90:16–17,

> Let Your work appear to Your servants,
> and Your glory to their children.
> And let the beauty of the LORD our God
>       be upon us,
> and establish the work of our hands for us;
> yes, establish the work of our hands.

Only God can establish works done by human hands and make them last forever. And only God can build the one church, that holy congregation which will never pass away. It is He who establishes each one of us in our appointed places as living stones within His eternal House: "you also, like living stones, are being built into a spiritual house to be a holy priesthood, offering spiritual sacrifices acceptable to God through Jesus Christ." (1 Peter 2:5, NIV)

## HIS TEMPLE, HIS BODY, HIS BRIDE

God's people are being built into a temple in which the Lord Almighty and the Lamb are pleased to dwell forever. Yet what a battle there has been over the building of this church throughout history! Jesus is coming back for a holy, sanctified, and purified church whose foundations were laid by the Lord Himself. That house will not be founded on human traditions, nor tied to any religious denomination. It will be built according to the pattern given in God's Word, Jesus Himself being the chief cornerstone.

In fact, God Himself will judge between those who truly follow Him, and those who merely have a form of religion—"having a form of godliness but denying its power." (2 Timothy 3:5) This is why it is so crucial that we be followers of the Lord and not of men, carefully studying God's word for ourselves. As Jesus warned in Mark 7:6–8 (NIV):

> Isaiah was right when he prophesied
> about you hypocrites; as it is written:
>  "These people honor me with their lips,
>   but their hearts are far from me.
>  They worship me in vain;
>  *their teachings are but rules taught by men.*"
> You have let go of the commands of God
> and are holding on to the traditions of men.
> (Emphasis added)

We have the great privilege of being called by God to build His eternal church while walking closely with Him. Everything else will pass away, but Jesus and His Bride will remain forever. To what then should we give our time and our strength but to building the Body of Christ? And what should be our greatest joy but that the Lord has His way among His people here on earth? As Hebrews 6:10 declares concerning those who give their lives to serve God's people, "For God is not unjust to forget your work and labor of love which you have shown toward His name, in that you have ministered to the saints, and do minister."

And what is the end of all true ministry (service) but that God's church—His people—be perfected in faith, character, and understanding? Consider again a passage we have referred to many times,

> And He Himself gave some to be apostles, some prophets, some evangelists, and some pastors and teachers, for the equipping of the saints for the work of ministry, for the edifying of the body of Christ, till we all come to the unity of the faith and of the knowledge of the Son of God, to a perfect man, to the measure of the stature of the fullness of Christ....
> (Ephesians 4:11–13)

What a beautiful end the Father has in mind for His children—that we all come "to the measure of the stature of the fullness of Christ...." If this then is the chief purpose of all the ministries listed in this passage, it is also the most important work of every disciple. Church buildings, committees, evangelistic associations and every other tool we use will pass away—it is the Lord and His people who will remain forever. My highest calling is to labor for the perfection of my brothers and sisters as members of Christ's Body, as well as for the transformation of my own soul into the image of Jesus.

How, then, do we go about building the Lord's church, His Body, in accordance with His pattern and will? As disciples of Jesus, we have the high privilege of being filled with the promised Holy Spirit. And it is that same Spirit who works in us now to make us members of one holy congregation: "For by one Spirit we were all baptized into one

body—whether Jews or Greeks, whether slaves or free...."
(1 Corinthians 12:13) The Spirit of God within us enables
us to take our places in the Body of Christ, as well as to
lay down our lives for the building up of the church. Al-
though there are many functions and giftings in which we
may serve, whether as prophets, teachers, or others, we do
not choose for ourselves what is appropriate. Instead, all
cleansed and yielded souls may freely approach their Father in Heaven to ask for those gifts and callings that are
appointed for them by the Spirit.

What richness, what variety of gifts and service the
Lord has appointed in His church! Contrast this with the
narrow, restrictive, traditional views of the church that so
many hold, and you will see why human traditions can
never express the full measure of eternal wisdom, glory,
and power that God intends to display in the Biblical
church. As Ephesians 3:10–11 declares, "His intent was
that now, through the church, the manifold wisdom of
God should be made known to the rulers and authorities
in the heavenly realms, according to his eternal purpose
which he accomplished in Christ Jesus our Lord." (NIV)

# 19    *The Bridegroom Cometh*

The world will neither see nor comprehend the marvels of God's eternal plan. Indeed, Jesus Himself states in Matthew 11:25, "I thank You, Father, Lord of heaven and earth, that You have hidden these things from the wise and prudent and have revealed them to babes." On the other hand, as Jesus spoke in Matthew 13:16, "But blessed are your eyes for they see, and your ears for they hear...." What a marvel that the Father has included us in His eternal plans for the church! Who is worthy of such blessings, of such privileges? Certainly none of us! Only as we let God have His way in our hearts and lives does He make us worthy of such gifts and callings—and teach us how to best make use of them, "for without Me you can do nothing." (John 15:5) We dare not run ahead of the Lord, but must seek Him diligently regarding His plans for the church, plans He formed from before the foundation of the world.

And because it is God who is the architect of all this, not us, another inescapable part of our life is learning to wait patiently for the Lord—to put our trust in Him and not in ourselves. If like me, you don't like waiting, get used to it! As disciples, salvation is not our work but Christ's. The Kingdom of Heaven is not our creation but the Lord's. And doing God's will is not about doing the best that we can, but seeking God until we obtain the mind of Christ—and then acting accordingly. As Zechariah 4:6 (NIV) declares, "This is the word of the LORD to Zerubbabel: 'Not by might nor by power, but by my Spirit,' says the LORD Almighty."

To repeat what we have noted before, faithfulness to God and to His will is more important than works, public acclaim, or even success—no matter how great. Paul warns us in 1 Corinthians 3:10-15,

> By the grace God has given me, I laid a foundation as an expert builder, and someone else is building on it. But each one should be careful how he builds. For no one can lay any foundation other than the one already laid, which is Jesus Christ.
>
> If any man builds on this foundation using gold, silver, costly stones, wood, hay or straw, his work will be shown for what it is, because the Day will bring it to light. It will be revealed with fire, and the fire will test the quality of each man's work. If what he has built survives, he will receive his reward. If it is burned up, he will suffer loss; he himself will be saved, but only as one escaping through the flames. (NIV)

Faithfulness requires absolute honesty on our part, regarding our motives, our failures, and our insufficiency. We must also persistently refuse to take to ourselves the glory and praise that belong only to our God. Let us pray as

David did in Psalm 139:23–24, "Search me, O God, and know my heart; test me and know my anxious thoughts. See if there is any offensive way in me, and lead me in the way everlasting." (NIV)

Finally, as disciples of Jesus, we must recognize that suffering is and will be part of our life in Christ. We should not seek it out as some religious people do, but neither should we flee from it, if God allows us to suffer for a season. Paul was one of the greatest builders of the church of all time, yet when Ananias did not want to pray for this new believer, the Lord told him, "Go, for he is a chosen vessel of Mine to bear My name before Gentiles, kings, and the children of Israel. For I will show him how many things he must suffer for My name's sake." (Acts 9:15–16) God often uses the suffering of His saints to build His church, as the long history of Christian martyrdom plainly reveals. As 1 Peter 1:3–9 states,

> Praise be to the God and Father of our Lord Jesus Christ!
>
> In his great mercy he has given us new birth into a living hope through the resurrection of Jesus Christ from the dead, and into an inheritance that can never perish, spoil or fade—kept in heaven for you, who through faith are shielded by God's power until the coming of the salvation that is ready to be revealed in the last time. In this you greatly rejoice, though now for a little while you may have had to suffer grief in all kinds of trials.
>
> These have come so that your faith—of greater worth than gold, which perishes even

though refined by fire—may be proved genuine and may result in praise, glory and honor
when Jesus Christ is revealed. Though you
have not seen him, you love him; and even
though you do not see him now, you believe
in him and are filled with an inexpressible and
glorious joy, for you are receiving the goal of
your faith, the salvation of your souls. (NIV)

We must keep our eyes continually fixed upon the eternal
prize before us, the salvation of our souls. Whatever the
trial or cost, the best policy in life is always to follow hard
after Jesus and do His will.

And if we suffer as a result of serving the Father and
building His eternal house, we share in Christ's sufferings.
Hebrews 12:2–3 declares that our Lord, "for the joy set
before him endured the cross, scorning its shame, and sat
down at the right hand of the throne of God. Consider
him who endured such opposition from sinful men, so
that you will not grow weary and lose heart." As an older
friend once said, "You cannot lose serving Jesus Christ."
Let us therefore serve Him with all our heart, soul, mind,
and strength—becoming lifelong disciples of the One to
whom all Heaven sings:

You are worthy to take the scroll,
    and to open its seals;
for You were slain,
and have redeemed us to God by Your blood
    out of every tribe and tongue
    and people and nation,
and have made us kings and priests
    to our God;
and we shall reign on the earth.
(Revelation 5:9-10)

# Acknowledgements

First of all, I would like to thank my gracious and loving wife, Pilar, without whose patience this book would never have been written. I am also grateful for the life and instruction of that long-term missionary to Colombia and lover of Jesus and His church, Mrs. Hannah Lowe. It was she who patiently confirmed and enlarged my understanding of the Biblical church. John McCandlish Phillips, a prayerful man of God who has been a spiritual father to me for several decades now, was both a guide and an inspiration. He was there ready to help every step of the way in the completion of this book, as well as with almost everything else I have written over the years.

I also want to thank others who helped immensely in the editing and completion of this work. Steve Ahn and Denise Chen read the manuscript early on in the process of its preparation and made valuable contributions. Yuna Lyons dedicated many hours to editing and improving the flow and clarity of the text. Philip Chamberlain, my brother-in-law and a Middle Eastern languages scholar at Yale, was particularly helpful in checking all references to Greek and Hebrew words. He also aided at numerous points with the clarity and accuracy of the wording of the text.

I also want to thank my dear friend, Andrew Burrows, who did the final editing of the book. He is a linguistics scholar, and a man with much wisdom and understanding. Dr. Prem Thomas, another close friend from my years at Yale, spent many long hours typesetting the text, endnotes, and bibliography in preparation for printing. Thanks also to Johnathan Caleb Rivers, a friend and talented graphic artist, who helped with preparing the cover of this book.

Finally, I thank the Lord for Paul, the apostle who has contributed so much to our understanding of the Biblical church. As King David got hold by prayer of the blueprints for God's earthly temple in Jerusalem, so Paul obtained from heaven the vision of God's plan for His eternal temple—the Church which is the Body and Bride of Jesus Christ. As he wrote in Ephesians 3:8–12:

> To me, who am less than the least of all the saints, this grace was given, that I should preach among the Gentiles the unsearchable riches of Christ, and to make all see what is the fellowship of the mystery, which from the beginning of the ages has been hidden in God who created all things through Jesus Christ; to the intent that now the manifold wisdom of God might be made known by the church to the principalities and powers in the heavenly places, according to the eternal purpose which He accomplished in Christ Jesus our Lord....

# *Notes*

## Chapter Prologue

1. (page xi) John 3:8, NIV.
2. (page xii) Ezekiel, chapter 1. NIV and KJV. Emphasis added.
3. (page xiii) 1 Corinthians 12. NIV. Emphasis added.
4. (page xiii) Romans 8:9. NIV
5. (page xiv) Ephesians 3:10. NIV
6. (page xiv) Isaiah 57:15. NIV
7. (page xiv) Revelation 14:4. NIV

## Chapter 1 Believers or Disciples?

1. (page 4) NT:4100, 4103. Strong 1890a, p. 58 *Note:* For the most part, "believe" appears in the Greek New Testament as a verb, i.e., an action. Biblesoft, Inc and International Bible Translators, Inc 2006
2. (page 5) NT:4103. Strong 1890a, p. 58
3. (page 5) OT:3928. Biblesoft, Inc and International Bible Translators, Inc 2006
4. (page 6) OT:565. Strong 1890b, p. 14
5. (page 8) NT:3101. Strong 1890c, pp. 266-7 and Strong 1890a, p. 45
6. (page 8) Bull 1957. I wrote down this quote years ago, and believe it is from this book. I have not since been able to confirm this.
7. (page 11) Spurgeon 2001, p. 260
8. (page 13) Hymn #156. Christian Publications 1936
9. (page 14) Spurgeon 2001, p. 204
10. (page 14) Hymn #144. Christian Publications 1936
11. (page 16) Hymn #191. Christian Publications 1936

12. (page 17) Elliot 1941–1955
13. (page 19) Ryden 1961, pp. 423–424
14. (page 20) Hymn #98. Christian Publications 1936

## Chapter 2 The Biblical Church

1. (page 26) Foxe 1563
2. (page 27) Tyndale 1530
3. (page 27) Merle d'Aubigné 1876, pp. 225-9

## Chapter 3 False Prophets

1. (page 32) Verploegh 1989, p. 206
2. (page 33) Reading for March 17. Chambers 1963, p. 77
3. (page 36) NT:5272. Strong 1890a, p. 74
4. (page 38) Edwards 1741

## Chapter 4 The Call of God

1. (page 43) NT:932. Biblesoft, Inc and International Bible Translators, Inc 2006
2. (page 43) Plural of NT:935. Biblesoft, Inc and International Bible Translators, Inc 2006
3. (page 44) NT:5590. Biblesoft, Inc and International Bible Translators, Inc 2006; Biblesoft, Inc 2006
4. (page 45) Plural of NT:2409. Biblesoft, Inc and International Bible Translators, Inc 2006
5. (page 46) Reading for June 21. Chambers 1963, p. 173

## Chapter 5 Freedom or Bondage?

1. (page 50) The etymology of "clergy" can be traced backwards through Old French (clergie, "clerics, learned men," since in the Middle Ages the clergy were among the few educated people), through Middle Latin (clericatus), and then through Latin (clericus, a priest)

as well as through the similar Greek term *klerikos* (an adjective meaning 'of the clergy' in hierarchical church jargon). The Latin *clericus* (from which the word *clerk*, or *cleric* as in clerical also derives), together with the Greek *klerikos* have their origins in the Greek word *kleros*, the only one of these words to actually appear in the Greek New Testament. While rare in the Greek New Testament, *kleros* ("lot, inheritance, portion") is frequent and prominent in the Greek Septuagint, the translation of the Hebrew Scriptures in common use during New Testament times. Harper 2012

2. (page 51) NT:2819. Strong 1890c, p. 637; Strong 1890a, p. 42; Biblesoft, Inc and International Bible Translators, Inc 2006

3. (page 51) Nicol 1915

4. (page 52) NT:3531. Biblesoft, Inc 2006

5. (page 53) NT:3534, νίκος or nikŏs, conquest or triumph. NT:2992, λαός or laŏs, people. Strong 1890a, pp. 50,44

6. (page 53) NT:3404. Strong 1890a, p. 48

7. (page 64) Spurgeon 2001, p. 228

8. (page 65) Fenchel 2009

## Chapter 6 Character and Community

1. (page 72) Spurgeon 1999, pp. 75–76

## Chapter 8 Will You Go with Jesus?

1. (page 88) NT:1577. Strong 1890a, p. 26

2. (page 88) OT:2416, OT:4150, OT:5712, OT:6951. Strong 1890c, pp. 215–6; Strong 1890a, pp. 38,63,85,102

3. (page 88) Reading for July 1. Chambers 1963, p. 183

4. (page 90) Jack Hayford makes a similar point. One of the reasons why God so desires each of us to worship Him is for our liberation, "because through it, you will be progressively liberated from yourself (which is life's worst bondage)." Hayford 2005, p. 46

5. (page 92) Reading for December 11. Chambers 1963, p. 346

CHAPTER 9 THE BLUEPRINT IN THE BIBLE

1. (page 95) Simpson 1890, p. 153
2. (page 99) Simpson 1890, p. 153

CHAPTER 10 APOSTLES

1. (page 101) NT:652. Biblesoft, Inc and International Bible Translators, Inc 2006
2. (page 103) NT:1978. Biblesoft, Inc and International Bible Translators, Inc 2006
3. (page 104) Marrat 1890

CHAPTER 11 PROPHETS

1. (page 111) NT:2919. Biblesoft, Inc and International Bible Translators, Inc 2006
2. (page 111) NT:1252. Biblesoft, Inc and International Bible Translators, Inc 2006
3. (page 115) Shakarian, Demos, Sherrill, John, and Sherrill, Elizabeth 1977, Chapter 1
4. (page 115) Knights Of Vartan Armenian Research Center 1996

CHAPTER 12 EVANGELISTS

1. (page 117) NT:2099. Biblesoft, Inc and International Bible Translators, Inc 2006
2. (page 118) Henry 1706, commentary on Acts 8:4–13
3. (page 120) Wiersbe 1989, p. 117
4. (page 120) Kyle and Todd 1998
5. (page 121) Penn-Lewis 1995, pp. 15–16
6. (page 122) Penn-Lewis 1995, p. 16

## Chapter 13 Pastors (Shepherds)

1. (page 125) NT:4166. Biblesoft, Inc 2006
2. (page 126) Strong 1890c, p. 917
3. (page 126) Strong 1890c, p. 343
4. (page 126) NT:4165. Biblesoft, Inc 2006
5. (page 127) NT:4165. Biblesoft, Inc 2006
6. (page 127) Strong 1890c, p. 343
7. (page 128) NT:1066. Biblesoft, Inc 2006
8. (page 128) NT:4165. Biblesoft, Inc 2006
9. (page 128) NT:4165. Biblesoft, Inc 2006
10. (page 129) Morris 1969, p. 959
11. (page 129) From *cardĭnālis*, "of or pertaining to a door hinge," which became the title of the "priests of the *hinge*." **Note**: Priests referred to the priests of the temple of Jupiter in Rome, and *hinges* referred to the hinges of the "holy doors" of that temple. Lewis, Charlton T and Short, Charles 1879
12. (page 131) Tyndale 1989, p. 285
13. (page 131) Tyndale 1989, p. 331

## Chapter 14 Teachers

1. (page 133) NT:1320. Strong 1890a, p. 23
2. (page 134) NT:2783. Strong 1890a, p. 42
3. (page 134) Ehrlich, Eugene et al. 1980, p. 305
4. (page 134) NT:1322. Strong 1890a, p. 23
5. (page 135) NT:1321. Strong 1890a, p. 23
6. (page 136) NT:1319. Strong 1890a, p. 23
7. (page 137) NT:1322. Strong 1890a, p. 23
8. (page 141) Reading for July 13. Chambers 1963, p. 195

## Chapter 15 Elders

1. (page 144) Biblesoft, Inc 2006
2. (page 144) NT:4245. Strong 1890a, p. 60
3. (page 146) Commentary on Philippians 1:1-2. Henry 1706
4. (page 148) Commentary on 1 Peter 5:1–4. Henry 1706

5. (page 149) Commentary on Philippians 1:1–2. Henry 1706
6. (page 149) Commentary on Philippians 1:1–2. Henry 1706

## Chapter 16 Deacons

1. (page 157) NT:1249. Strong 1890a, p. 22

## Chapter 17 Other Gifts

1. (page 168) NT:2941. Strong 1890a, p. 44
2. (page 172) Taylor 2009

## Chapter 18 Thy Will be Done

1. (page 176) Lewis 1994, pp. 174–5

# Bibliography

Biblesoft, Inc (2006). *Biblesoft's Interlinear Transliterated Bible.*

Biblesoft, Inc and International Bible Translators, Inc (2006). *Biblesoft's New Exhaustive Strong's Numbers and Concordance with Expanded Greek-Hebrew Dictionary.*

Bull, Geoffrey (1957). *When Iron Gates Yield.* London: Hodder & Stoughton Ltd.

Chambers, Oswald (1963). *My Utmost for His Highest.* New York: Dodd, Mead & Company, Inc.

Christian Publications, comp. (1936). *Hymns of the Christian Life.* Harrisburg, Pennsylvania: Christian Publications, Inc.

Edwards, Jonathan (July 8, 1741). *Sinners in the Hands of an Angry God.* Christian Classics Ethereal Library. URL: http:// www.ccel.org/ccel/edwards/sermons.sinners. html (visited on 03/19/2008).

Ehrlich, Eugene et al., comp. (1980). *Oxford American Dictionary.* New York: Oxford University Press.

Elliot, Philip (1941–1955). *Papers of Philip James Elliot - Collection 277.* Billy Graham Center. URL: http://www. wheaton.edu/bgc/archives/faq/20.htm (visited on 02/13/2012).

Fenchel, Steve (Mar. 14, 2009). "'The Priestly Walk,' Entering the Holy Place in the Tabernacle". A message given at Congregation Sha'ar Adonai. New York, New York.

Foxe, John (1563). *Fox's Book of Martyrs*. Winston ed. note: Compiled from Fox's Book of Martyrs, and other authentic sources. Chicago, Philadelphia, Toronto: The John C. Winston Co. URL: http : / / www . gutenberg . org / files / 22400 / 22400 - h / 22400 - h . htm # Page _ 19 (visited on 02/14/2012).

Harper, Douglas. *Online Etymology Dictionary*. URL: http : / / www . etymonline . com / index . php (visited on 01/16/2012).

Hayford, Jack (2005). *Manifest Presence*. Grand Rapids, Michigan: Chosen Books.

Henry, Matthew (1706). *Commentary on the Whole Bible*. PC Study Bible Formatted Electronic Database. Biblesoft, Inc.

Knights Of Vartan Armenian Research Center (Apr. 3, 1996). *Fact Sheet: Armenian Genocide*. The University of Michigan-Dearborn. URL: http : / / www . umd . umich . edu / dept / armenian / facts / genocide . html (visited on 02/14/2012).

Kyle, Ted and John Todd, comp. (Sept. 1998). *A Treasury of Bible Illustrations*. Bible Illustrations Series 2. AMG Publishers.

Lewis, Charlton T and Short, Charles (1879). *A Latin Dictionary*. Oxford: Clarendon Press. URL: http : / / www . perseus . tufts . edu / hopper / text ? doc = Perseus : text : 1999 . 04 . 0059 : entry = #6777 (visited on 02/14/2012).

Lewis, C. S. (1994). *The Horse and His Boy*. New York: Harper Trophy.

Marrat, Jabez (1890). *The Apostle of Burma. A Memoir of Adoniram Judson, D.D.* Toronto: Methodist Mission Rooms.

Merle d'Aubigné, J.H. (1876). *History of the Reformation in Europe in the time of Calvin*. Vol. 5. 8 vols. New York: Robert Carter & Brothers. URL: http : / / www . archive . org /

details / historyofreformat187605merl (visited on
02/05/2012).

Morris, William, ed. (1969). *The American Heritage Dictionary
of the English Language*. Boston: American Heritage Publishing Co., Inc and Houghton Mifflin Company.

Nicol, Thomas (1915). *The Old Latin Version*. In: *International
Standard Bible Encyclopedia*. Ed. by James Orr. URL: http :
//www.bible-researcher.com/oldlatin.html (visited on 02/05/2012).

Penn-Lewis, Jessie (1995). *Prayer and Evangelism*. Fort Wash-
ington, Pennsylvania: Christian Literature Crusade.

Ryden, E.E. (1961). *The Story of Christian Hymnody*. Rock Island, Illinois: Augustana Press.

Shakarian, Demos, Sherrill, John, and Sherrill, Elizabeth
(June 1, 1977). *The Happiest People on Earth*. Hodder
& Stoughton Religious.

Simpson, Albert B. (1890). *A Larger Christian Life*. New York:
The Christian Alliance Publishing Co.

Spurgeon, Charles H. (1999). *Spurgeon's Sermons*. Vol. 3. Grand
Rapids, Michigan: Baker Books.

— (2001). *Morning and Evening*. New Kensington, Pennsylvania: Whitaker House.

Strong, James (1890a). *Dictionary of the Greek Testament*.
Nashville, Tennessee: Abingdon.

— (1890b). *Dictionary of the Hebrew Bible*. Nashville, Tennessee: Abingdon.

— (1890c). *The Exhaustive Concordance of the Bible*. Nashville,
Tennessee: Abingdon.

Taylor, James Hudson. *Christian Quotes by James Hudson Taylor*. Daily Christian Quotes. URL: http : / /
dailychristianquote.com / dcqtaylor . html (visited on 04/22/2009).

Tyndale, William (1530). *A Pathway into the Holy Scripture.* URL: http://www.newmatthewbible.org/pathway.html (visited on 02/14/2012).

— (1989). *Tyndale's New Testament.* Ed., with an introd., by David Daniell. New Haven and London: Yale University Press.

Verploegh, Harry, comp. (1989). *Oswald Chambers: The best from all his books.* Vol. 2. Nashville, Tennessee: Thomas Nelson, Inc.

Wiersbe, Warren (1989). *The Bible Exposition Commentary: New Testament.* Vol. 2. Colorado Springs, Colorado: Chariot Victor Publishing.

# ABOUT THE AUTHOR

Mr. White, the son of a Congregational minister, was reared in various small New England towns. He graduated from Masconomet Regional High School in Boxford, Massachusetts. After completing three semesters at Yale University he withdrew, unable to afford the costs, and worked in home improvement contracting in Yonkers for several years. Later he returned to Yale to complete his degree, graduating with honors in 1987 with a major in History, focusing on the Middle East. His senior essay, *A Time to Favor Zion: the Jews of Jerusalem 1825-1850*, was commended by the Chancellor of Tel Aviv University.

Having earned his M.A. in Education in 1991 at Teachers College/Columbia University, Mr. White taught mathematics and history at public and private high schools, including Scarsdale High School, the Greenwich Country Day School, the Masters School in Dobbs Ferry, and for twelve years, at the Convent of the Sacred Heart on 91st Street in Manhattan. Honors received while in education include being nominated in 2003 and 2006 to *Who's Who Among America's Teachers*, and being named Outstanding Teacher in the Upper School at Convent of the Sacred Heart in 2005. As of July 1, 2007, he retired from teaching mathematics to go into full-time evangelism.

Mr. White is a member evangelist of the Proclamation Evangelism Network, and also of the Next Generation Alliance of the Luis Palau Evangelistic Association. He has spoken in numerous open-air outreaches in various parts of New York City, including Wall Street, Broadway, Flushing Meadow Park, Times Square, and Columbus Circle. He has held evangelistic concerts every summer since

2003 at the Naumburg Bandshell in Central Park, New York City, and now also at the Jones Beach Boardwalk Bandshell on Long Island. He also speaks in churches in various parts of the city.

Beginning with an invitation in April 2004 from the president of CEDECOL, the consortium of evangelical churches of Colombia, Mr. White has made more than twenty evangelistic journeys to Colombia. He has spoken in evangelistic outreaches and campaigns in Bogotá, Cali, Bucaramanga, Santa Marta, Ipiales, Sogamoso, Piedecuesta, and many other cities in Colombia. In May 2010, he held his first evangelistic campaign in Tulcan, Ecuador. He has appeared numerous times on radio and television in Colombia. In March 2006, he was a featured speaker at the First Colombian National Congress of Evangelists in Bogotá, presenting on the theme "The Passion of the Evangelist."

He was a leader in campus Bible studies at Yale for many years, and took part in Bible studies at Princeton for several years. In recent years, he has been a regular guest speaker at Yale, Columbia, and various other universities in the northeastern United States. He has also helped organize the city-wide One Cry university prayer gatherings in New York City for the last few years together with Jeremy Story, President of Campus Renewal Ministries. An ordained minister, a singer and songwriter, he is the author of more than thirty sacred songs.

He and his wife, Pilar, have four sons, Joseph, Jacob, Matthew, and Nathaniel.

www.cnwhite.org
cwhiteevan@yahoo.com

## Colophon

This book was typeset with LaTeX using the memoir, microtype, and fontspec packages and the LuaTeX engine. The text uses Arno Pro with headers in Gill Sans; both are from Adobe.

CPSIA information can be obtained at www.ICGtesting.com
Printed in the USA
BVOW071757130313

315382BV00002B/3/P